PAPs
An A-Z of particularly Attractive Ideas

With the author's best wishes

David H

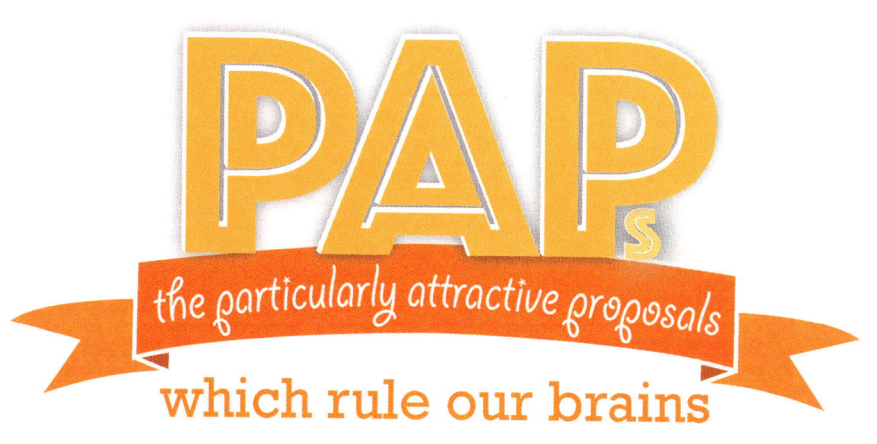

PAPs
the particularly attractive proposals
which rule our brains

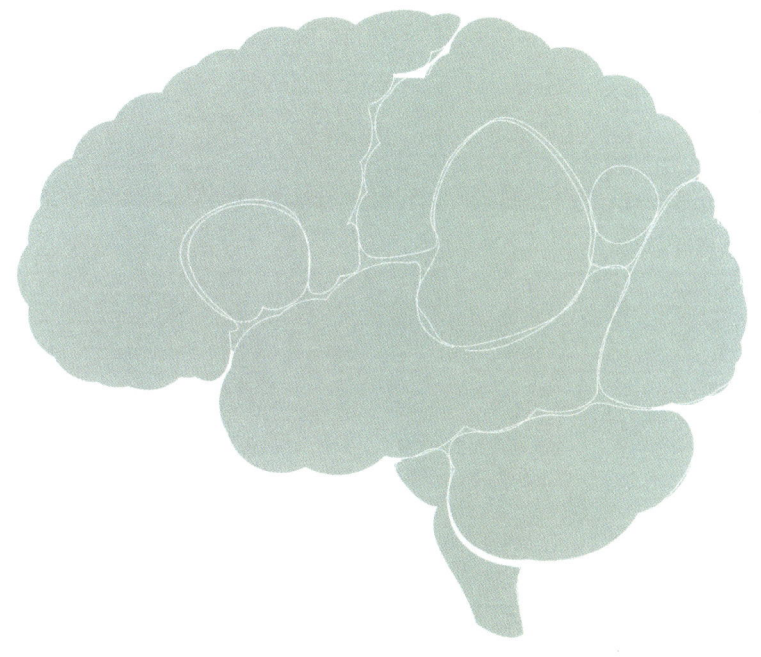

David Hamilton

The Partick Press
St Andrews 2016

PUBLISHED IN SCOTLAND BY THE PARTICK PRESS

Copyright © David Hamilton 2016

No part of this book may be reproduced without the
express permission of the copyright owner.

Design by George Bowie
Supported and Printed by CreateSpace

PAPs

PARTICULARLY ATTRACTIVE PROPOSALS

Some of the human race, some of the time, are attracted to irrational, even daft, ideas. They catch our attention and get support in spite of a lack of evidence and indeed many reasons for scepticism. These ideas are found scattered throughout all human activities, and it is convenient to pluck them from their niche location and here gather them together as a group. These are the 'Particularly Attractive Proposals' and they can be given the new acronym PAPs. This also hints that their ready acceptance comes through giving some motherly comfort.

This A-Z list is of those PAPs which are better known. Many are held dear, because many would like them to be true. PAPs are found are all over the place and the extent of such beliefs is confirmed by opinion polls which show, for instance, popular support for extra-terrestrial life, or astrology or that UFOs exist. Belief in clairvoyance or telepathy is widespread, even though scientists have given up trying to pin down these claims in the lab; 'there may be something in it' is the charitable public's verdict. Serious persons earnestly scan Loch Ness in Scotland looking for the Monster, or hunt for Bigfoot in the Pacific Northwest. Belief in witches has declined (in the West), but is still stuck at 26% support in American polls. Major PAPs include the comforting, widespread faith beliefs, notably in Heaven (65% support in the polls). We even seek them in our reading and publishers know which particularly attractive plots will appeal, particularly in fiction, and authors eagerly provide them. We listen credulously to urban myths, too good to be false, and pass them on. In medical care, confident nutritionists successfully tempt us to 'de-tox' from mythical, non-existent toxins.

None of these PAPs are rational; instead they appeal to the imaginative bit of our mind. To obtain traction in our brains, they exploit faith – belief without proof. Most PAPs are innocent and beguile us but do not lead us astray. But some can be dangerous. Against all reason, many believe there is a quick way to riches, and after trusting risky financiers, suffering follows. Some of us cling to charismatic but flawed preachers and leaders who let us down in the end.

Nor do we learn. When each new get-rich plan fails and another financial crisis rocks the world, it is soon ruefully pointed out that such bubbles come round regularly, appearing anew when the memory of the last disaster has faded. In other human endeavours, even in medicine, other PAPs return cyclically.

Why are we vulnerable? Man emerged after a long evolutionary process. The brain of *Homo sapiens* emerged from an ancient, simpler animal nervous system and added in this new ability to think, plan and create. It seems that this extra, powerful faculty has a curious fault, namely an attraction to ideas which are not rational. The defect does not seem to have any survival value, and there has not yet been enough time for the notoriously slow process of natural selection to eliminate this weakness for PAPs.

Sir Francis Bacon spotted the defect early, and in 1620 put it succinctly when calling them the 'Idola tribus' – the idols of the tribe – lamenting that *false notions, which are now in possession of the human understanding, and have taken deep root therein, not only so beset men's minds that truth can hardly find entrance.*

These 'false notions', are unstoppable and it seems they will always be attractive. PAPs are not innate, but we make them welcome when encountered. They come into our brain from outside, and at birth, there is a tolerant slot in the brain waiting for them to arrive.

Here are many of the PAPs, as an A-Z list available for browsing. There is a substantial scholarly literature relating to them individually and accordingly further reading has been added in the footnotes. All that remained was the acronym to draw them all together.

David Hamilton
St Andrews 2015
davidhamiltonstandrews.com

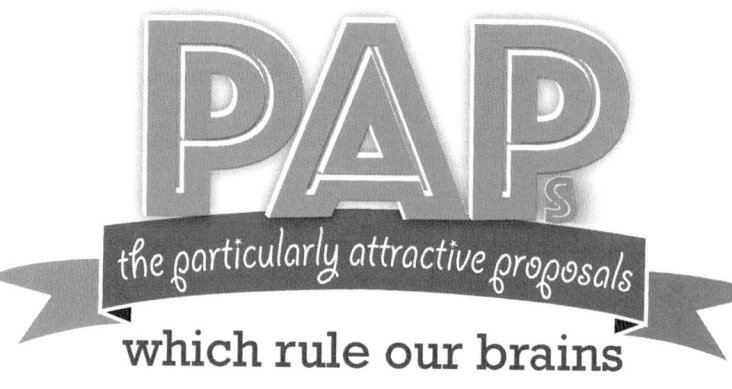

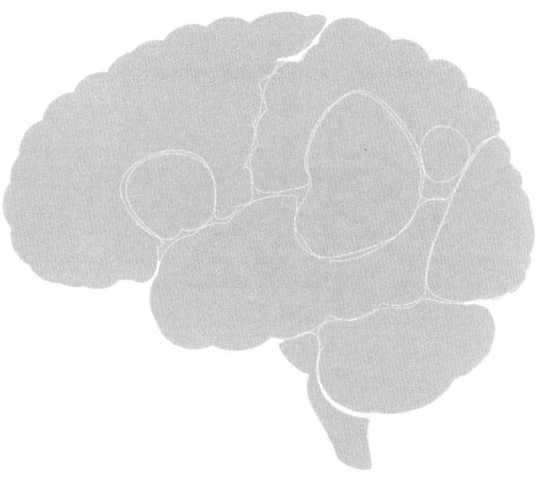

PAPs
the particularly attractive proposals
which rule our brains

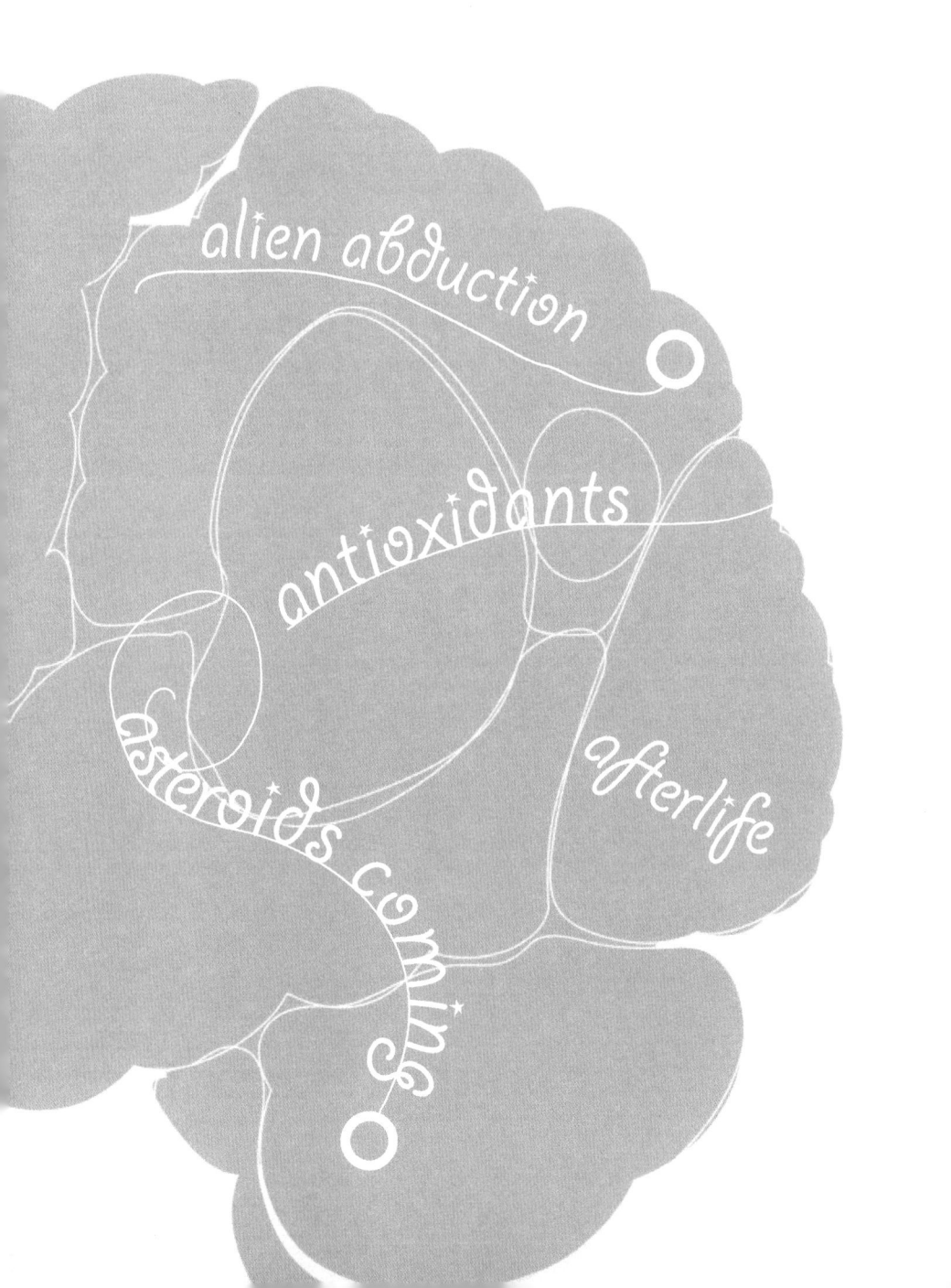

alien abduction

antioxidants

afterlife

asteroids coming

A

AFTERLIFE is the continuation of the body or soul after death and features in most religions, with dispatch, according to merit, to a *Heaven* (q.v.) or *Hell* (q.v.). Reincarnation, also according to merit in the earlier earthly life, is believed in by many.

ALICORN BUBBLE was one of the first financial manias. Increasingly extravagant prices were paid until the mid-1700s for powder allegedly made from the horn of the *Unicorn* (q.v.). It foreshadowed many similar financial follies to follow – the Darien Scheme, the Tulip Mania, *South Sea Bubble* (q.v.), *Railway Mania* (q.v.), Wall Street Crash, DotCom Bubble, and Subprime Crisis. See also *Get Rich Quick*.

ALIEN ABDUCTION has been confidently reported by some, who are unshakable in their accounts. Others explain it as fantasy or false memory.[1]

AMAZONS A legendary race of female warriors featuring in Greek mythology, but also found in other histories up to the 4th century B.C.[2] Widely used as a *Literary Trope* (q.v.).

ANTHROPOMORPHISM is the attractive idea that animals have human traits, including intelligence, bravery, loyalty, nobility (lions), or even cunning (wolves). A frequent theme in traditional tales, not only for children, it is also a favourite with publishers, requiring appropriate illustrations, starting with Lewis Carroll. Animated film and video games greatly increase the scope for use of transformed animals.

ANTI-CHRIST A belief in some religions in an opponent to Christ (other than the less personally hostile *Devil/Satan* (q.v.)). Biblical prophecies say the Anti-Christ will make one last stand before Christ's Final Coming. Some living persons were considered by the Catholic Church to be this threatening person, naming Emperor Frederick II and Tsar Peter the Great: protestant reformers have named the Pope as the Antichrist.

---

[1] John E. Mack *Abduction: Human Encounters with Aliens*, Simon and Schuster 1996.

[2] Adrienne Mayor *The Amazons: Lives and Legends of Warrior Women Across the Ancient World*, Princeton University Press 2014, and Lyn Webster Wilde *On the Trail of the Women Warriors*, Constable 1999.

ANTIHEROS lack heroic qualities and are troubled figures. Found from Greek literature onwards, these alienated figures struggle against the world of which they are not a part, nevertheless attracting interest and even sympathy.[3] The fiction of the 1950s and 1960s used 'outsiders' as central characters. In sport, the antihero is not a team player and may challenge the leadership. In professional wrestling an antihero is choreographed into the action, but after early ominous success, Good triumphs in the end.

ANTIOXIDANTS sound like (good) chemicals since they reduce the (bad) free radicals in the cell by preventing oxidative reactions. The long list of antioxidants includes many vitamins. They are praised in the alternative medical sector, and by high street nutritionists, for their help in dealing with heart disease, cancer, aging and much else. No firm evidence for this assistance has emerged.

ARTHURIAN LEGEND This legendary 5th/6th century king saved Britain, against the odds, from the Saxons, and also from malign supernatural forces. He ran a gracious court at Camelot and his chivalrous Knights of the Round Table were ever-ready to do noble deeds. The fictional genre of Arthurian Romance was established by the addition of Galahad, Sir Lancelot (lover of Queen Guinevere), Merlin (the *Wizard* q.v.) and the *Holy Grail* (q.v.). Use of the myth peaked in 19th century, helped by the works of Tennyson and Wagner.

ASTEROID, THREATS OF A favourite Internet topic and in fiction, raising fear of doomsday collisions of comets with the earth.[4] NASA's ever-calm Near-Earth Object Program steadily rebuts each new alarm. See also *Velikovsky, Immanuel.*

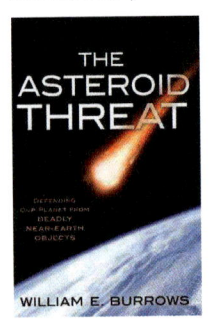

ASTROLOGY is the ancient belief that the position of celestial objects, notably the planets, influence world events. Many newspapers still carry astrological advice in horoscopes and the belief has adherents and influence in high places.[5]

ATLANTIS, LOST ISLAND OF Plato's fictional island continent proves to be a durable *trope* (q.v.), with multiple uses, and continual speculation that the story is historically accurate. The myth was kept alive by Thomas More and by Francis Bacon in his *New Atlantis* (1624). See *Islands, Legendary.*

---

[3] David Simmons *The Anti-Hero in the American Novel*, Palgrave Macmillan 2008.

[4] William E. Burrows *The Asteroid Threat*, Random House 2014.

[5] Roger B. Culver and Philip A. Ianna *Astrology, True or False? A Scientific Evaluation*, Buffalo 1988.

ATONEMENT is a particularly admirable position, making amends for wrongdoing, not only setting the record straight, but inviting forgiveness. It is a prominent strategy in some religions and a favourite theme in chat shows.

AUTOINTOXICATION is the persistently attractive premise in alternative medicine that the body creates internal toxins which cause disease and debility. The pioneer was Sir Arbuthnot Lane, who carried out colon removal in the 1920s to counter this threat. The *Colon* (q.v.) and its contents are still regarded with suspicion by some, notably those practitioners offering colonic lavage.[6]

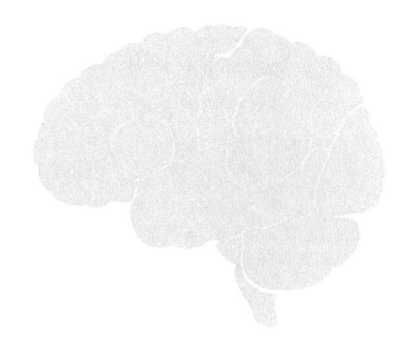

---

[6] Ann Daly *Fantasy Surgery 1880-1930*, Rodopi 1997.

find bigfoot

boosting the immune system

brain gyms

bastards over the hill

B

BADNESS see *Letting the Badness Out*.

BACON, SIR FRANCIS, in his *Novum Organum* (1620) identified the 'Idola tribus' (idols of the tribe) which were 'false notions' which 'so beset men's minds that truth can hardly find entrance.' He had got it: these are the PAPs.

'BASTARDS OVER THE HILL' is the verdict needed to show that neighbouring nations, or rival teams, or those in other religions or ethnic groups are beneath contempt.[7] It is a potent cause of neighbourly feuds, violence, and war. Related to the PAP *Stereotypes* (q.v.).[8]

BED REST Until relatively recently, bed rest was advised during any illness, or after surgical operations or childbirth. Instead, it was a potent cause of deep venous leg thrombosis, chest infections and mental depression, as well as giving costly in-patient hospital care.
It seemed a good idea at the time – i.e. a PAP lasting for many centuries.

BIG CATS Large feral wild cats are repeatedly sighted in Britain notably in Scotland, Devon and Surrey, but none have been captured, nor their remains found.[9] Clearly a cryptid-PAP of the *Bigfoot* (q.v.) type.

BIGFOOT is a man-like creature described from early times by the native inhabitants of the Pacific North-west, and one still enthusiastically sought by investigators. Their negative findings do not discourage using the theme in fiction and films.[10] Similar hominid PACs (Particularly Attractive Creatures) are widely found in other countries, including the Yeti in the Himalayas, Chuchunya in Siberia, Moehau in New Zealand, Yowie in Australia and Scotland has the Grey Man of Ben MacDhui.[11] See *Cryptids*.

---

[7] Vamık Volkan *The Need to Have Enemies and Allies* Jason Aronson, Lanham 1988.

[8] See for instance the nasty Scottish clan rivalries in Alexander Macgregor *The Feuds of the Clans* Mackay, Stirling 1907.

[9] Graham J. McEwan *Mystery Animals of Britain and Ireland*, Robert Hale 1986.

[10] Joshua Blu Buhs *Bigfoot: The Life and Times of a Legend*, Chicago University Press 2009.

BLINDSPOT The claim that particularly unattractive prejudices to race, colour, religion, age, etc persist in the subconscious mind, even of those who have consciously and scrupulously accepted liberal ideas. These alleged residual blindspots are uncovered by the psychologist's 'Implicit Association Test'.[12]

BLOOD, YOUNG The PAP persists that youthful blood has rejuvenating power when transfused into the old or infirm. This strategy was first used by a Pope in 1490 and more recently by Kim Il-Song (1912-1994) the former North Korean dictator. The PAP is not dead. See also *Vampires*.

BLOODLETTING was thought to be a Good Thing for several thousand years, and is easily classified as a PAP. It was thought to act by *Letting the Badness Out* (q.v.), the highly-embedded eternal medical PAP.

BLUEGRASS MUSIC has a limited range of Particularly Anguished Plots – hardship, love (lost and found), and death.[13]

BOOSTING THE IMMUNE SYSTEM This favourite medical PAP seeks to increase the level of the *general* defences of the body against disease, notably infection and cancer. Although niche immunisation against specific organisms by vaccines is highly successful, general stimulation of immunity has not been obtained by conventional medical therapy. However, practitioners of alternative medicine regularly claim their strategies are successful.

BOYER, PASCAL the French philosopher can be quoted with approval – 'innate mental systems make human beings predisposed to certain cultural beliefs, notably in the supernatural.' His book is *Religion Explained* (2002).

BOORSTIN, DANIEL J. in his *The Image: A Guide to Pseudo-events in America* (1960) he pointed to the lure of putting an extra gloss on reality. He quoted a mother's response to admiration of her new baby – 'that's nothing – you should see his photo.'

BRAIN TRAINING, BRAIN GYMS follow the seductive idea that the brain's mechanisms are not fully used and hence performance can be improved. The concept has not been supported in mainstream science, but is a favourite in self-help publications and commercial products.[14]

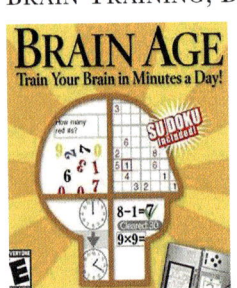

---

[11] Marjorie Halpin and Michael M. Ames *Manlike Monsters on Trial* 1980, and Affleck Gray *The Big Grey Man of Ben Macdhui*, Edinburgh 1994.

[12] Mahzarin R. Banaji *Blindspot: Hidden Biases of Good People*, Delacorte 2013.

[13] Jimmie N. Rogers *The Country Music Message*, Arkansas 1989.

[14] See the video game *Dr. Kawashima's Brain Training: How Old Is Your Brain?* and *Brain Gym: Teacher's Edition* (revised 2010).

BRINKLEY, JOHN R. (1885-1942) This Texas quack gland-grafter successfully exploited the PAP that goat tissue would confer the sexual prowess of that animal.[15]

BROWNE, SIR THOMAS added weight to *Francis Bacon's* (q.v.) earlier encouragement of critical thinking. In Browne's 1646 book *Pseudodoxia Epidemica* (q.v.) he listed many PAPs, collected together as the 'Vulgar Errors of the Day'.

BRUNONIANISM The Scottish physician John Brown (1735-1788) viewed most diseases as resulting from general over- or underperformance of the body (high or low 'excitability'). If low, general stimulation was needed.[16] His simple system was widely adopted in Europe in the Romantic Period, and elements of it remain in some current PAPs – see *Manichean Dualism*. See also *Boosting the Immune Response* and *Romanticism*.

BUBBLE – a name used for the recurring financial crises following massive investments of the wrong sort. See *Alicorn Bubble*.

BUBBLE ACT passed in 1720 sought to limit public investment after the scandal of the *South Sea Bubble* (q.v.) that year. It did control speculation and was in force until 1825. After repeal, the immediate effect was a revival of financial crises, notably the *Railway Mania* (q.v.) of the 1840s.

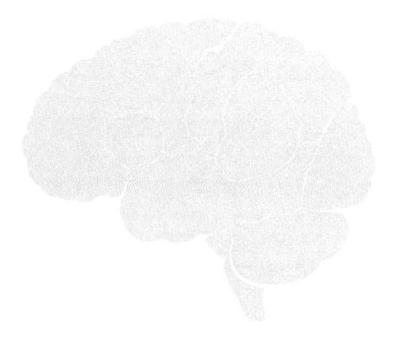

---

[15] R. Alton Lee *The Bizarre Careers of John R. Brinkley,* Kentucky University Press 2002.

[16] *Medical History* Supplement no. 8, 1988.

cellist's scrotum

conspiracies abound

chosen people

creationism

clairvoyane

'CANCER SCARE'/'CANCER SURVIVOR' is a claim favoured by celebrities and their publicists. Recovery in rehab from drugs or alcohol is less attractive.

CARGO CULTS During WW2, natives on the Pacific islands observed the remarkable airborne influx of goods for the American troops. After the War, local cult leaders taught that the cargos would return if they used invocations and accordingly maintained the abandoned landing strips.

CASAUBON, REV EDWARD In George Eliot's *Middlemarch* (1874) this cleric sought to show that all the world's myths came from a single corpus of ancient knowledge (i.e. PAPs). He dies before proving his claim. Seeking for such seductive 'theories of everything' has been called the 'Casaubon Delusion' by Anthony Campbell.

CAST-AWAY, THE is a favourite literary *Trope* (q.v.) in fiction, and life on desert islands have featured regularly in fiction from *Robinson Crusoe* (1719) onwards to the *Life of Pi* (2001).

CASUS BELLI the plausible cynical public excuse needed to enter a war already agreed and planned.

CELLIST'S SCROTUM was an ailment mentioned by a musician in a lighthearted letter to the *British Medical Journal* in 1980. Though a spoof, news of the disability spread, being a PAP too good to be false. 'Guitarist's nipple' is however a real nuisance to these virtuosi.

CENTRAL CASTING gives a supply of suitable actors to fit niche roles.

'CHANGE' a favourite and attractive political slogan - see *Political PAPs*.

CHOMSKY, NOAM (b 1928) taught that children have an innate knowledge of grammatical structure and hence that our social, intellectual and habitual behaviour is built-in. This is the opposite of the concept of the mind as a *Tabula Rasa* (q.v.), a view now out of favour.

CHOSEN PEOPLE is a belief that a nation or movement has been chosen by God to Do His Work on Earth. Ethno-centrism is involved, namely the belief that the Chosen People's values, being superior to those of others, hence finds favour with God.

CLAIRVOYANCE is the gaining of knowledge of events which have not been directly experienced. Practitioners claim to be able to foresee the future and in opinion polls, 26% of Americans believe in this power.

CLUSTERING of non-rational beliefs is common. Believers in one, such as *UFOs* (q.v.), tend to believe in others, like the *Paranormal* (q.v.).

COLON A well-known PAP is that the colon is a danger to the body, allegedly harbouring dangerous poisons and bacteria; hence the colon has to be purged. See *Autointoxication*.

COOK BOOKS A profitable PAPublishing genre.

COMMON MISCONCEPTIONS – see the long list in Wikipedia. The earliest list came from *Sir Thomas Browne* (q.v.) in 1646.

CONFIRMATION BIAS is the preference, shown even by scientists, to use evidence confirming the original proposal and shun data disproving it. Related to this, shortly after the announcement of bold new concepts which are shown much later to be wrong, other reports confirming it rapidly appear for a while. See *Sheepish Tendency* and *Woozle Effect*.

CONSPIRACY THEORIES are particularly attractive to some, and range from the belief in the power of secret organisations, such as the Freemasons, to allegations that the truth on major historical events is being concealed. Events given alternative sinister explanations include JFK's assassination, the 9/11 attack, the origin of AIDS, the death of Diana, the Holocaust and America's moon landing.[17] These theories thrive on the inevitable unexplained anomalies in the main story. This is an active area in publishing. See *Illuminati* and the *X-files*.

CONTRARIAN thinking, reflexly and regularly opposes the majority view, often taking on unpopular positions. At its best, in science it may hasten emergence of new *Paradigms* (q.v.) to replace old dogma. In publishing, contrarian works sell well. See the more strident single issue *Denialism* (q.v.).

'CONVENTIONAL WISDOM' is a term popularised by the economist John K. Galbraith for the ideas accepted at any time by the majority. He suggested that these are attractive to the mind, give comfort and hence resist replacement.

---

[17] Theodore Ziolkowski *Lure of the Arcane: The Literature of Cult and Conspiracy*, Johns Hopkins 2014, Christopher Hodapp and Alice Von Kannon *Conspiracy Theories and Secret Societies for Dummies*, Wiley 2008 and Peter Knight *Conspiracy Culture*, Routledge 2001. For a list of conspiracy theories, see Wikipedia.

[18] Damian Thompson *Counterknowledge: How We Surrendered to Conspiracy Theories, Quack Medicine, Bogus Science, and Fake History*, W.W.Norton 2008.

COSY MYSTERY FICTION a niche genre of 'feel good' fiction set in small town locales where the amateur sleuth, after encountering discouragement from locals, solves a major crime or identifies a murderer living in plain sight. The action has little violence or sex.

'COUNTERKNOWLEDGE' A phrase used by the crime novelist Stav Sherez to point out the increasing acceptance of demonstrable untruths (i.e. PAPs) and the unfortunate assistance of the Internet and pliant publishers.[18]

CREATIONISM The Biblical idea that the earth was created by God in seven days is still attractive to many, against the evidence.[19]
A Gallup Poll in 2011 showed 46% Americans accepted that God created man 'in the last 10,000 years'. Other religions accept a similar sudden arrival of our world.

CRUNCH OF 2008 – one of the alternative names for the serious financial *Bubble* (q.v.) of the time.

CRYPTIDS/CRYPTOZOOLOGY is the study and hunt for animals whose existence has not been proven – see *Bigfoot* and *Loch Ness Monster*.[20]

CULTIC MILIEU a term coined by the sociologist Colin Campbell in 1972 for the 'cultural underground space' occupied by participants supporting *Clusters* (q.v.) of non-rational, even bizarre beliefs.[21]

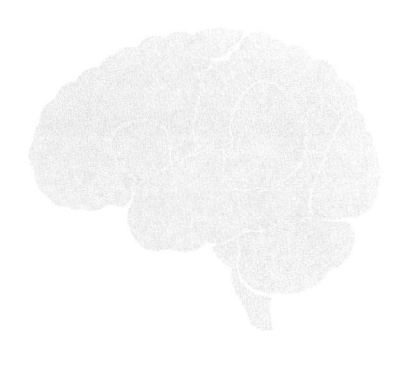

---

[19] Ronald L. Numbers *The Creationists: From Scientific Creationism to Intelligent Design*, Harvard U.P. 2006 and Arthur McCalla *The Creationist Debate*, Continuum 2006.

[20] Loren Coleman, and Jerome Clark, *Cryptozoology A to Z*, Simon and Schuster 1999 and Daniel Loxton and Donald R. Prothero *Abominal Science: Origins of the Yeti, Nessie and Other Famous Cryptids*, Columbia U. P. 2013.

[21] Jeffrey Kaplan and Heléna Lööw (eds) *The Cultic Milieu: Oppositional Subcultures in an Age of Globalisation*, AltaMira Press 2002.

detox

buy dot-coms

devil

deluge happened

D

DARIEN SCHEME was a risky Scottish financial *Bubble* (q.v.) in the 1690s backed by much of Scotland's national funds and which ended in disaster: it hastened the Union of Parliaments with England.

DAVID AND GOLIATH story was the biblical triumph of an *Underdog* (q.v.). It is also noted in other 'asymmetric' situations, notably guerrilla warfare, and as a literary *Trope* (q.v.) in which a worthy, likable rebel triumphs against the power of the rich or the bureaucracy.[22]

DELUGE, THE
A legend of a great flood which nearly destroyed mankind appears in the traditions of many cultures, with Noah's Ark added in the Bible and the Quran.[23] So pervasive is the flood legend that it might not be a PAP, but all attempts to link it to historical floodings have failed.

DENIALISM is the refusal to believe the reasonable findings of others on major issues of the day, often creating sustained controversy and publicity. Denial is prominent in the discussion on evolution, the Holocaust, and climate change.[24] See the less strident *Contrarian* (q.v.) stance. *Scepticism* is a temporary cautious, healthy stance taken while awaiting closure of a debate.

DETOX involves a superficially attractive idea that in normal health there can be a temporary build up of 'toxins' from time to time and that these need removal. In spite of the wide acceptance of this PAP, particularly in the alternative medical world, no such toxins exist. See *Letting the Badness Out* and *Focal Sepsis*.

---

[22] Malcolm Gladwell *David and Goliath: Underdogs, Misfits and the Art of Battling Giants*, Little Brown 2013.

[23] Alan Dundes (ed) *The Flood Myth*, University of California Press 1988.

[24] Michael Specter *Denialism: How Irrational Thinking Hinders Scientific Progress, Harms the Planet and Threatens Our Lives*, Penguin 2009 and Michael Shermer and Alex Grobman *Denying History*, University of California Press 2009.

DEVIL 70% Americans believe in both Hell and the Devil and only 21% are resolute disbelievers.[25] The Hajj pilgrimage to Mecca by Moslems involves a ritual 'stoning of the Devil'. See *Hell*.

DOOMNIC(K)S are those fond of making dire warnings of imminent world crises – global warming, overpopulation, resource depletion, war, famine and disease.[26] See also *Prophets*.

DOT-COM BOOM See *Bubbles*.

DRACULA This grimly attractive gothic horror figure remains a favourite in fiction, theatre and film. See *Blood, Young*.

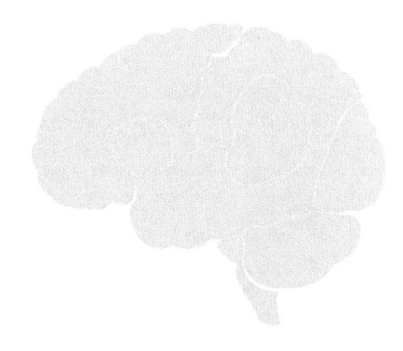

---

[25] Henry Ansgar Kelly *Satan: A Biography*, Cambridge UP, 2006.

[26] Christopher Booker *The Real Global Warming Disaster*, Continuum 2013.

E

EL DORADO Tales heard in South America by the Spanish conquistadores in the early 1500s described a distant wealthy city of gold and encouraged many expeditions, including one by Sir Walter Raleigh. The name is used to signify the futility of attempts to *Get Rich Quick* (q.v.).

ELECTRICAL MACHINES were much favoured as medical treatment in Victorian times, together with magnetism.[27] Less clear at present is the benefit of TENS machines (transcutaneous electrical nerve stimulation) in pain relief. The Cochrane Library's assessment of its use says sternly that 'new studies of rigorous design and with adequate numbers of patients are needed before any evidence-based recommendations can be made for patients or health professionals.'

END IS NIGH The melancholy *fin de siècle* view regularly appearing that progress is ceasing for The World (q.v.), or for Science,[28] Nature,[29] the West,[30] and History.[31] See also *Doomnik*.

END OF THE WORLD (EOTW) this prediction was a theme in earliest mythology, and is still offered, with some even offering a date. Millenarist Joanna Southcott (1750-1814), the English prophetess, predicted that the world would end in 2004. Disappointed earlier believers were the followers of the Massachusetts prophet William Miller who sold their belongings in good time to deal with his forecast of 21 March 1844, shortly after recalculated by him to be 22 October. Charles Russell of the Jehovah's Witnesses named 1914 and William Branham (the Pentecostalist (d 1965)) said the year 1977 was revealed to him as the end by angels. March 1982 was predicted in *The Jupiter Effect* (1974), and Jerry Falwell the televangelist in 1999 cautiously said 'soon'. More recent anticipations include 2015 (by Rabbi Chaim Kanievsky), 2020 (psychic Jeane Dixon),

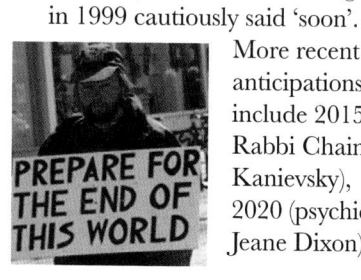

---

[27] Gerrit L. Verschuur *Hidden Attraction: The Mystery and History of Magnetism*, Oxford 1996.
[28] John Horgan *The End of Science*, Basic Books 2015.
[29] Bill McKibben *The End of Nature*, Bloomsbury 2003.
[30] Paul Kennedy *The Rise and Fall of Great Powers*, Vintage Books 1987.
[31] Francis Fukuyama *The End of History*, Free Press 1992.

2021 (according to the Mariners Church, California), 2026 (Messiah Foundation International), 2060 (favoured a while back, by Sir Isaac Newton), and 2120 was proclaimed by both Adnan Oktar, the Islamic creationist, and Said Nursî, the Turkish Muslim theologian.[32] The evangelist Jim Bakker, after release from four years in prison, sold survival kits for the Next Coming. The End was usually predicted to be preceded by major events and disasters, some also believing that the *Antichrist* (q.v.) will make a brief appearance. See *www.bible.ca/pre-date-setters* for a useful list of now-survived EOTW dates. A happier EOTW climax is Teilhard de Chardin's *Omega Point* (q.v.) – to be reached by steady improvement in the human race.

ENRON 'too big to fail' couldn't be bust, could it? This huge $111 billion award-winning company, well thought of by investors and analysts, went bankrupt in 2001. It was sustained only by a cynical creative-accounting fraud.

ESCHATOLOGY see *End of the World*.

ESTABLISHMENT, THE a term coined by the journalist Henry Fairlie and used in Anthony Sampson's *The Anatomy of Britain* (1962) to suggest Britain was run by a self-replicating inner group of the 'right people' who had control and made all the major decision.[33] A benign *Conspiracy Theory* (q.v.).

ETERNAL LOSER, THE
A poignant figure in politics, sport, fiction and soap operas, who gains the sympathy of observers.

'EUREKA' MOMENT - 'I have found it.' A favoured view that scientists have sudden revelations, the first incident claimed being Archimedes' insight in his bath, realising that the water displaced by an irregular object would equal its volume. Delighted, it is said he ran naked through the streets of Syracuse, announcing his finding. Sceptics point out that the first record of his story did not appear for 200 years. Many savants deny such revelations, which are much sought after by science journalists.

EVANGELIST'S PAPs. See *Afterlife* and *Heaven*.

EXORCISM 42% Americans believe that possession by the Devil can occur and that removal is required and is possible. Exorcism is a variety of the PAP *Letting the Badness Out* – (q.v.)[34]

---

[32] Tom McIver *The End of the World: an Annotated Bibliography*, McFarland 1999 and Paul Boyer *When Time Shall Be No More: Prophecy Belief in Modern American Culture*, Harvard UP 1992.

[33] Owen Jones *The Establishment and How they Get Away with It*, Allen Lane 2014.

[34] Brian P. Levack *The Devil Within: Posession and Exorcism in the Christian West*, Yale 2013.

EXCEPTIONALISM The internally attractive idea that a nation, society or institution is unusual and hence exempt from many of the normal rules or constraints. This can include claims to be chosen by God. See *Chosen People*.

'EXTRAORDINARY POPULAR DELUSIONS AND THE MADNESS OF CROWDS' was published in 1841 by the Scottish journalist Charles Mackay. It ridiculed economic folly like the *Darien Scheme* (q.v.) and the *South Sea Bubble* (q.v.). The book also described many other PAPs including 'National Delusions', 'Peculiar Follies', 'Philosophical Delusions' and *Witch-hunts* (q.v.), condemning the belief in Alchemy, *Prophecy* (q.v.), and fortune-telling. Present-day writers on recent cyclical financial follies still quote his analysis – 'men think in herds and go mad in herds and recover only slowly'. The book is still in print.

EXTRATERRESTRIAL LIFE on other planets is believed in by 41% of Americans in recent Gallup Polls.[35]

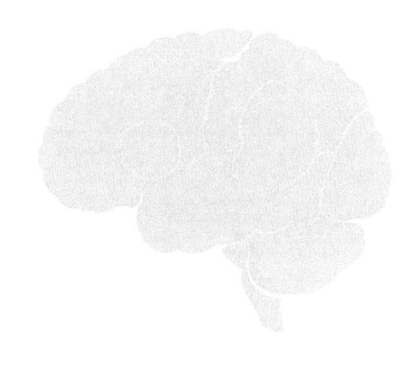

---

[35] Don Lincoln *Alien Universe: Extraterrestial Life in Our Minds and the Cosmos*, Johns Hopkins UP 2013.

focal sepsis

fairy tales

free radicals

feel good factor

F

FACE MASKS were introduced into surgery to protect the patient from the surgeon's breath. Now, simple nonabsorbent paper masks are widely used in the hope of protecting a person from the air around – manifestly impossible.

FAIRY TALES usually aimed at children, have a short, educative and entertaining narrative, without a clear locus, often involving nonhuman beings, animals and magical events. Danger looms but following a crisis, there is a happy ending.[36] There is no claim that the events happened, unlike legends. Many national variants on core fairy tale themes are found and they are occasionally used to support nationalism. New variants on these tales can sell remarkably well.

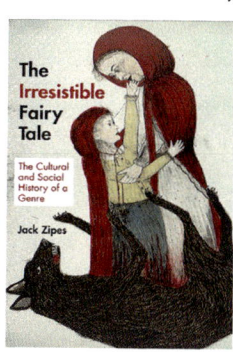

FALSE MEMORY see *Recovered Memory*.

FEEL-GOOD (F-G) an uplifting mood delivered by events, the media and fiction. All musicals seek the F-G factor. F-G films are favoured at times of national difficulty – the US Depression or post-war Britain.

FIDEISM is the view that faith – i.e. belief without proof – is superior to reason in establishing some kinds of truth. To a fideist, rational analysis of some PAPs, particularly those associated with the religions, is inappropriate, as faith alone gives them authority. See *Intuition*.

FOCAL SEPSIS A recurring attractive idea that danger lurks in organs inside the body. Notable suspects have been the tonsils, adenoids, appendix and colon, being allegedly responsible for debility, arthritis and even mental illness. Surgical removal has been resorted to in the past – see *Colon*, *Detox* and *Letting the Badness Out*.

FOOD ALLERGIES The UK's regulatory body (NICE) says only one in five claimed food allergies are clinically significant.

---

[36] Marina Warner *Once Upon a Time A Short History of Fairy Tale*, Oxford 2015, Jack Zipes (ed) *The Oxford Companion to Fairy Tales*, Oxford 2010, and Rosalind Kerven *English Fairy Tales and Legends*, National Trust 2008.

PARTICULARLY ATTRACTIVE PROPOSALS

FOUR HOURS SLEEP – said to be the reduced need of heroic persons or celebrities.[37]

fMRI a sophisticated human brain scanning technique which lights up the area of the brain being used by the topic of thought. When listening to statements believed to be true, the ventromedial area of the brain cortex brightens up: hence storage of PAPs is in this area.

FREE RADICALS are cellular chemicals said by some to be causative, in excess, not only of cancer and heart disease but aging. Treatment by antioxidants notably vitamins E and C would be logical if the danger was accepted by main-stream science, which it is not.

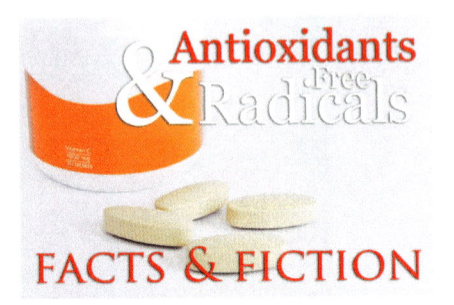

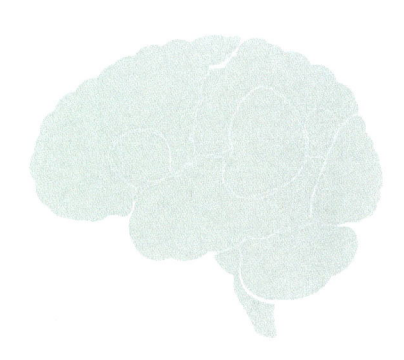

---

[37] Alan Derickson *Dangerously Sleepy: Overworked Americans and the Cult of Manly Wakefulness*, University of Pennsylvania Press, 2014.

G

GALBRAITH'S (JOHN KENNETH) important book *The Great Crash* concluded that *'not only fools but quite a lot of other people are recurrently separated from their money in the moment of speculative euphoria.'* [38] Galbraith blamed the banking system, but it seems the fault was with the citizens. As each new scheme for gaining riches emerges, another PAP is invoked to minimise fears – 'It's different this time.' [39]

GENES as cause of everything, is a particularly attractive idea, since it removes personal accountability.

GET RICH QUICK Hope for immediate riches is one of the oldest and saddest PAP. For a few of the famous occasions on which many sensible people were parted from their savings by plausible schemes, see *Bubbles, Darien Scheme, South Sea Bubble, Ponzi Scheme* and *Pyramid Scheme*.

GHOSTS are the manifestations of departed humans, often inhabiting a particular location. One third of Americans believe in haunted houses but serious ghost-hunting faded in the West by the mid-1900s. [40]

GOD(S) are the person(s) believed to have created the world and continue to supervise all its activities. A 2011 Gallup Poll showed that 92% of Americans 'believed in God' slightly down from 1944 figure of 96%. 19% of these believers had some doubts: only 7% interviewed were convinced God does not exist. [41]

GOD, HELPED BY A claim made by many, including politicians, celebrities and sportsmen. Assistance was asserted by Sarah Palin (on her presidential bid in 2012), the 9/11 survivors, and rulers like Corazon Aquino. In sport, those claiming assistance were Eric Liddell (gold at the 1924 Olympics), Jerry Yang (World Series poker champion 2007) and golfer Gary Player (Masters winner 1961). Jose Mourinho, London's Chelsea football club manager, believes that results of penalty shoot-outs were determined

---

[38] John Kenneth Galbraith *The Great Crash*, Pelican 1961.

[39] Linda Stratmann *The Crooks who Conned Millions*, Sutton 2010.

[40] Ronald C. Finucane *Appearances of the Dead and Cultural Transformation: A Cultural History of Ghosts*, Prometheus 1996 and Jenny Uglow (ed) *The Chatto Book of Ghosts*, London 1994.

[41] Michael Shermer *The Believing Brain*, Times Books 2011.

by God. Hitler believed God looked after him, notably in escaping the assassination attempts, and US Navy sniper Chris Kyle claimed his bullets were on occasions guided by God.

GOD, PUNISHMENT BY
US evangelist Jerry Falwell thought the AIDS epidemic was God's punishment for tolerance of homosexuals and Rev Pat Robertson similarly considered Hurricane Katrina was a punishment for America's sins. The UK's Bishop of Carlisle suggested in 2007 that the local UK floods were God's response to moral decline.

GOLDACRE, BEN the UK Journalist involved in tireless exposure of the PAPs used and pedalled by the alternative medicine sector.[42]

GiTWAD (Great in Thought, Word and Deed): the high-mindedness said to be possessed by *Heroes* (q.v.).

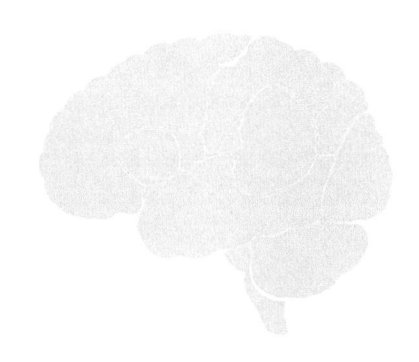

---

[42] Ben Goldacre *Bad Science*, Harper 2009.

H

A Happy Ending is essential in fictional works, with the hero escaping from danger, or finding God or himself, and after winning the girl, 'living happily ever after.'

Haunted Houses In US Gallup Polls, 37% believed in such inhabitations by the departed. Sceptics point to other mundane explanations of the scary experiences regularly reported.[43]

Heart, Touching of This curious prohibition among surgeons against touching the human heart persisted into the 20th century and held back any proposals for heart surgery. Touching was alleged to cause immediate fatal irregular beating of the heart. Once the PAP was discredited, the heart proved to be one of the more robust human organs.

Heaven features in most religions as a place of pleasure, above the sky, for reception of the *Souls* (q.v.) of deserving dead persons. Supervised by God and his angels, admission may be denied, leading to diversion to *Hell* (q.v.). Residence in either is thought in most religions to be temporary until resurrection or reincarnation as a new person.[44] Gallup Polls in America showed that Heaven attracted 81% believers with only 11% resolute disbelievers.

Hell in the Abrahamic traditions is seen as final resting place for punishment of the soul of sinners, the final transfer there perhaps being delayed until the Last Day. It is usually depicted as a hot place beneath the ground supervised by the eternal Devil.[45] US Gallup Polls show a belief in Hell at 61%, lower than *Heaven* (q.v.). Born-again Christians have a more lively belief in Hell at 89% and Heaven at 97%.

Heros For Thomas Carlyle, hero worship is 'the noblest emotion, the germ of all religion.'[46] But the dangers of hero-worship is image-adjustment to be 'an actor in the script written by others'.[47]

---

[43] Yvette Fielding and Claran O'Keeffe *Ghost Hunters* Hachette (2011).

[44] Anthony DeStefano *A Travel Guide to Heaven*, Image 2005.

[45] Salomon Kroonenberg *Why Hell Stinks of Sulphur: Mythology and Geology of the Underworld*, Reaktion 2014 and Kaufmann Kohler *Heaven and Hell in Comparative Religion*, Kessinger 2003.

[46] Thomas Carlyle *On Heros, Hero-worship and the Heroic in History* 1841.

[47] Archie Brown *The Myth of the Strong Leader*, Bodley 2014.

In mythology, heroes are dynamic, virile, semi-divine, solitary men (and occasionally women) who take on daunting tasks, defeat the enemy, or save a nation, often appearing after a recall from banishment. Achilles was the first hero. Sporting heroes are a feature of childhood comics.[48] See *GiTWAD*.

HE WAS INNOCENT/FRAMED/ UNFAIRLY EXECUTED is a favourite mission, one not always wrong, of journalists, relatives and authors, attempting to show that justice had erred: such missions offer attractive publications.[49]

HIGH PRESSURE OXYGEN (Hyperbaric Oxygen, in medical treatment) is a curious PAP which regularly beguiles even orthodox medicine and has a firm hold in alternative medicine circles. Oxygen is a Good Thing and providing more of it in this way comes round with a cycle of about thirty years, when a new generation has no memory of the negative verdict earlier. It is, however, essential for treating decompression sickness or carbon monoxide poisoning.

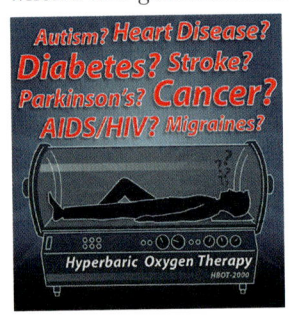

HOAX Because PAPs are readily accepted without suspicion, hoaxes are regularly successful when using PAP themes. See for instance the internet site supporting the Dihydrogen Monoxide Research Organisation and the studies of this ubiquitous environmental hazard. Other agencies seeking members or offering support are the Lake Michigan Whale Watchers, the Federal Zombie Protection Agency, The Brain Transplant Clinic and Save The Guinea Worm.[50] Hoaxes which ridiculed unpopular philosophical fashions include the influential Sokal Hoax.[51] Hoax pharmaceutical advertisements and websites include those promoting Strivor for the fictitious Motivational Deficiency Disorder (which affects 1 in 5) and Havidol® (avafynetyme HCl) for 'dysphoric social attention consumption deficit anxiety disorder'. See also *Cellist's Scrotum*.

HOLY GRAIL The idea persists that a drinking vessel used at Christ's last supper survived and has magical powers. Prominent in Christian writings and other legends, it was the theme of a flurry of successful books from 2000.[52]

---

[48] Lucy Hughes-Hallet *Heroes: Saviours, Traitors and Supermen*, Harper 2004.
[49] See *Innocence Network* UK.
[50] Alex Boese *The Museum of Hoaxes*, Dutton 2002.
[51] Alan D. Sokal and Jean Bricmont *Fashionable Nonsense*, Picador 1998.
[52] Giles Morgan *The Holy Grail*, Chartwell Books 2009.

HOLY/SACRED BOOK A single source revered by a religion, organisation or political movement, and considered inspired or even infallible – The Bible, The Koran, Mao's Red Book, Hitler's Mein Kampf, etc.

HOMEOPATHY is an alternative medical system based on the plausible idea that 'like drives out like', and the practitioners use small doses, plus hitting the container while making the necessary dilutions. Critics' calculations suggest that only water remains after these extreme dilutions.

HOOD, ROBIN This charismatic outlaw laudably robbed the rich to pay the poor, and has enduring fame in popular culture and fiction.[53] Rob Roy MacGregor enjoys similar attention as a Scottish folk hero.[54]

HUMANISM An early PAP – a belief dominant in late mediaeval times that Romans and Greeks had done it all, and that all that remained was to discover the texts.

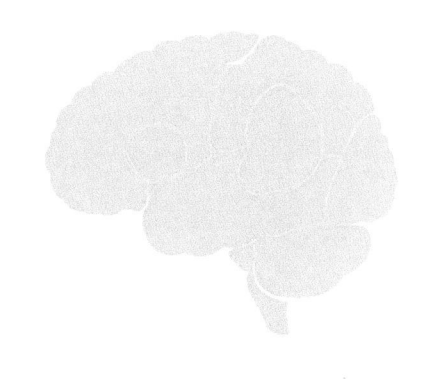

---

[53] David Baldwin *Robin Hood: The English Outlaw Unmasked*, Amberley 2010.

[54] David Stevenson *The Hunt for Rob Roy: The Man and the Myths*, Edinburgh 2004.

islands, lost

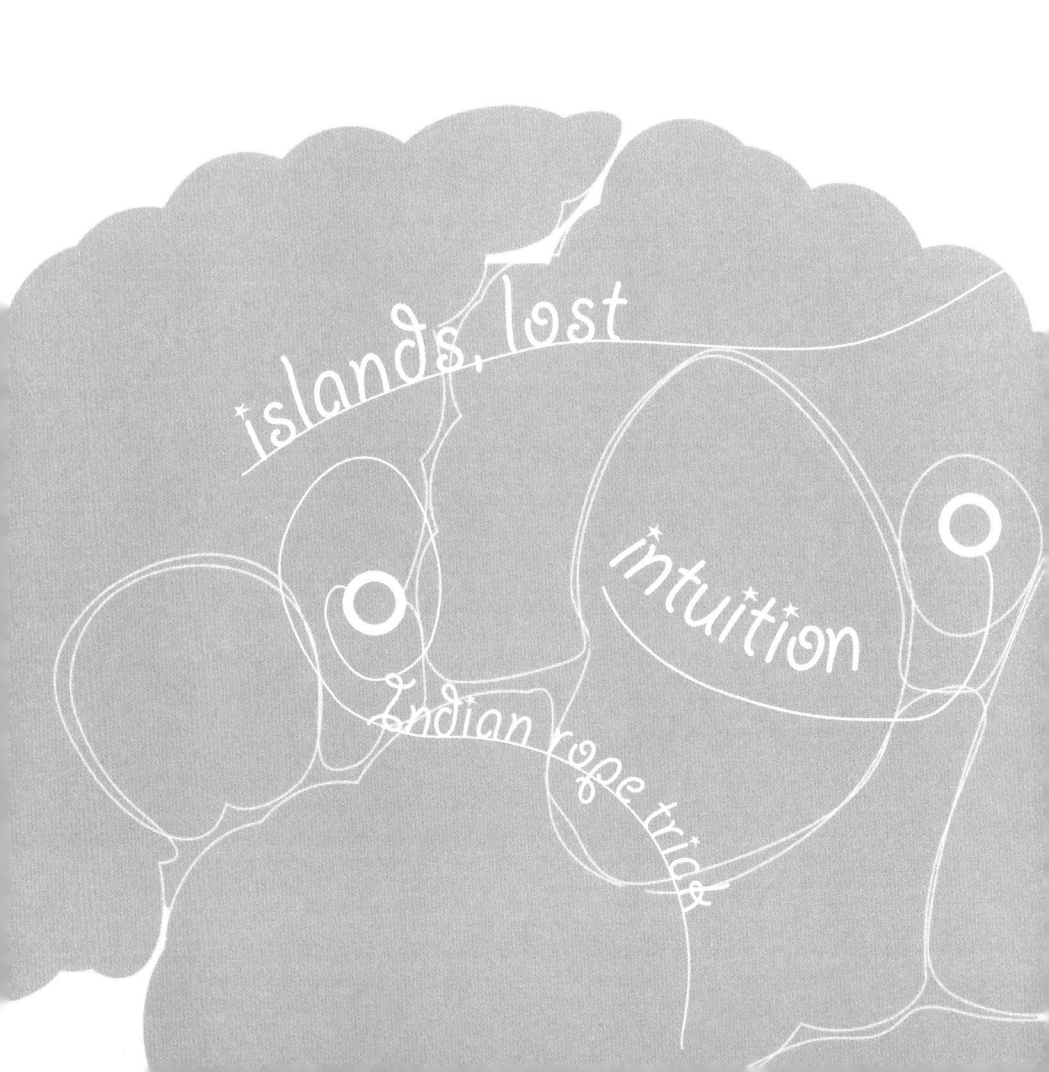

intuition

Indian rope trick

I

ILLUMINATI A *Conspiracy Theory* (q.v.) which holds that world events are controlled and manipulated by an ancient *Secret Society* (q.v.) of Bavarian origins which was suppressed in the late 1700s as a threat to the state. It is alleged that it survived and went on to orchestrate a variety of historical events, notably the Battle of Waterloo, the French Revolution and John F. Kennedy's assassination.

INDIAN ROPE TRICK Travellers told of how Indian street entertainers could induce a rope to rise into the sky, up which a boy assistant climbs and then disappears. The reports came from friends of friends and credible eyewitness accounts could not be traced. Stage illusionists popularised belief in the trick, which took on the life of a PAP.[55] See *Levitation*.

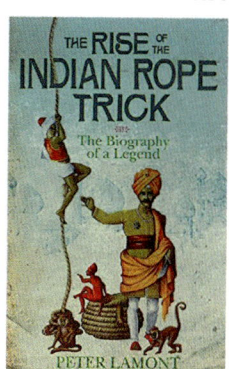

INTUITION, widely believed to exist, is the gaining of knowledge without the usual extended process of reasoning. Belief in it comes from personal anecdotes. Scientific proof that useful insights can be thus obtained without recourse to the relevant evidence or rational thought would be difficult to obtain, and the usual verdict is sceptical.[56]

ISLAND, MAROONED ON This attractive fictional theme used the potential inherent in the castaway scenario, and included *Gulliver's Travels*, *The Coral Island*, *Treasure Island*, *Robinson Crusoe*, and *The Swiss Family Robinson*. More sinister events occur in H.G. Wells' *The Island of Doctor Moreau* and *Lord of Flies*. The successful BBC radio talk show *Desert Island Discs* dates from 1942 offering castaway celebrities the chance to reminisce. *Monkey Island* was a successful pioneer computer game series.

ISLANDS, LEGENDARY AND LOST a favourite theme in myths and legends.[57] See *Atlantis*.

---

[55] Peter Lamont *The Rise of the Indian Rope Trick: The Biography of a Legend*, Little, Brown 2005.

[56] William Duggan *The Seventh Sense*, Columbia 2015.

[57] Umberto Eco *The Book of Legendary Lands*, MacLehose Press 2015 and Donald S. Johnson *The Phantom Islands of the Atlantic*, Avon Books 1998.

liverish

lost lands

loch ness monster

JKL

JORDON CAMELS President Nixon and his entourage, visiting Jordon, found that the camels assembled as background to a photo shoot were in fact (mono-hump) dromedaries. Since the Middle East image could not be authentic without dual-hump camels, some were quickly flown in from Egypt.

KIM JONG-UN (born 1983), the present leader of North Korea, is one of the last national heads of state to be credited with multiple heroic qualities. Even in golf, on his first visit to the links, he scored multiple holes-in-one. See *Hero*.

LAKE AND LOCH MONSTERS Belief in these animals is widespread in many cultures, immediately suggesting they are the PAP variant PAC (Perennial Appearing Creatures).[58] The best known is the *Loch Ness Monster* (q.v.) in Scotland. Major monsters in Canada include 'Ponik' in Lake Pohenegamook ('The Loch Ness of Quebec') and 'Champ' in Lake Champlain; the Altamaha River in Georgia has the 'Altamaha-ha'; the 'Nahuelito' inhabits an Argentina lake and 'Selma' has been sighted in Norway's Lake Seljord. These *Cryptids* (q.v.) all usefully sustain local tourism.

LANE, SIR WILLIAM ARBUTHNOT was the elegant pioneer of the PAP that the human colon is a source of poisons and a cause of disease. He encouraged avoidance of constipation and could even advocate surgical removal. His PAP continues to support the use of colonic lavage. See also *Letting the Badness Out*.

'LAW OF ATTRACTION' states that 'positive thinking' brings in its rewards – a view first enunciated by the late 19th century New Thought Movement based on the teachings of Phineas Quimby (1802-1866). The Law featured strongly in similar teachings later, notably those of Norman Vincent Peale (1898-1993), Dale Carnegie and similar American inspirational writers and evangelists.[59] See *Positive Thinking*.

'LESSONS LEARNED' The particularly attractive verdict after each of the West's financial crashes or *Bubbles* (q.v.). However, the core weakness, the lure of greed, is never learned. See *Get Rich Quick*.

---

[58] Michel Meurger *Lake Monster Traditions: a Cross-cultural Analysis*, TBS 1988 and Peter Costello *In Search of Lake Monsters*, Anomalist Books 1974.

[59] Steven Watts *Self-Help Messiah: Dale Carnegie and Success in Modern America*, Other Press 2013.

LETTING THE BADNESS OUT (LBO) is the PAP explaining use of many human medical therapies, old and new, aiming to release toxic influences from inside the body. These routines used bloodletting plus induced vomiting and bowel evacuation, all aimed at ridding the body of harm. Colonic lavage and *Detox* regimens (q.v.) have similar aims and successfully appeal to this deeply embedded PAP. Similar strategies have a role in ancient non-Western medicine. See also *Focal Sepsis* and *Exorcism*.

LEVITATION by Eastern holy men during meditation was widely believed to be possible. It was usually reported via the FoF (friend of a friend) route and has never been witnessed under careful study; it can be staged fraudulently. See also *Indian Rope Trick*.

LIVERISH an ancient often self-diagnosed vague debility alleged to come from the liver. It is sometimes more specifically, if unhelpfully, termed a 'sluggish liver' in alternative medical circles.

LOCH NESS MONSTER In spite of the longstanding claims for the existence of a creature in this Scottish Highland loch, close scientific surveillance has given no positive sightings. Hoax claims have been staged in the past and alternative explanations include floating driftwood or surfacing seals. There are regular sightings of Nessie at start of tourist season, and he/she would be at least 100 years old. Similar less confident claims come from other Scottish Highland lochs – Lochs Fyne, Urabhal, Arkaig, Eil, Lochy, Assynt and Morar.[60] See *Cryptids*.

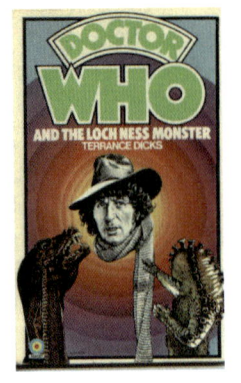

LOCKE, JOHN (1632-1704), the English philosopher, unhelpfully proposed that the new-born human brain is a *'tabula rasa'* (q.v.) i.e. a 'blank slate', and that we obtain our understanding entirely from bringing in experience through the senses. He soon had the powerful support of Scotsman David Hume (1711-76). This view is no longer held, as the brain's PAP slot suggests. See *Nativism*.

LOST LANDS Early explorers believed that beyond the known boundaries lay magical lands and that expeditions would find them eventually. The tales about *El Dorado* (q.v.) attracted many. In fiction, Conan Doyle's *The Lost World* was located in the Amazon rainforest. The Swiss Lötschental valley in the Bernese Alps remained cut off until the early 20th century and was viewed as a blessed area. See *Islands, Lost*.

---

[60] Henry H. Bauer *The Enigma of Loch Ness*, Illinois UP 1986.

M

MACK, JOHN E. As one of a number of academics supporting fringe beliefs, this tenured Harvard psychiatrist and Pulitzer Prize winner published his supportive book *Abduction: Human Encounters with Aliens* (1994). The University's investigation tolerantly concluded that 'Harvard can afford to have a couple of oddballs.'[61]

MADOFF, BERNIE This charismatic American operator of a *Ponzi Scheme* (q.v.) plausibly offered investors high regular returns on their investment. Having been chair of New York's Nasdaq Stock Market and running a legitimate broking business, he was widely trusted, yet operated a massive $65 billion fraud from the mid-1980s.[62] See *Get Rich Quick*.

MANICHEAN DUALISM extends the ancient Persian Manichaeism religion's core tenet of a struggle between Light and Darkness, and sees vivid dualism elsewhere – Yin and Yang, Good and Evil, Galenical Warm and Cold, even the human ambiguity as in the Jekyll and Hyde story. See also *Brunonianism*.

MARTYR Those admired for dying for a cause, notably their religion.[63] The term now includes those risking danger in pioneering work with unknown hazards – such as radiology.

'MEDIAEVAL' The word, when attached, conveys an unfortunate image of this time as being one of sustained ignorance and barbarity.[64]

MELIORISM the attractive view that the human race and society is making steady progress as a result of liberal democracy.

MEME Richard Dawkins' neologism for ideas, phrases or behaviour which spread in communities through speech, imitation or writing. Though similar to genes in replication and mutation, they are more rapidly established. Their spread and establishment is greatly assisted when they are PAPs.[65] See also *Trope*.

---

[61] Michael Lucas *Los Angeles Times*, 4 September 2001.

[62] Erin Arvedlund *Madoff: The Man Who Stole $65 Billion*, Penguin 2009.

[63] Candida Moss *The Myth of Perception: How Early Christians Invented a Story of Martyrdom*, Harper 2013.

[64] Johannes Fried *The Middle Ages*, Belknap Press 2015.

[65] Richard Dawkins *The God Delusion*, Black Swan 2007.

MILLENIARISM the belief in many religions that a golden age lasting 1,000 years will ensue after the return of Christ and will end with the final judgement.[66]

MILLS AND BOON the UK publisher, produce short romantic novels featuring a small range of recycled plots, usually featuring women attracted to initially unattainable alpha males, with a happy ending. Over a million books are sold per month and after three months, unsold stock is returned and pulped.[67]

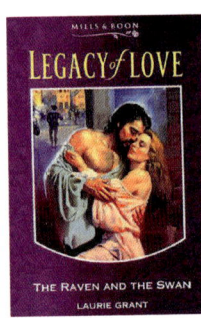

MIRACLE CURES Unexplained cures at Lourdes and elsewhere are less frequently claimed than before, but such shrines are still attractive to pilgrims.[68]

MONSTERS, MYTHICAL are found in every culture and its literature as PAPs – dragons, serpents, sea serpents, the unicorn and many others.[69]

MYTHS are traditional tales, not based on fact (unlike some legends) which have an ancient role in human culture. Their content enhance spirituality, give moral instruction and entertain. When gathered from throughout the world, the myths show surprising similarity, and use many PAPs as *Tropes* (q.v.).[70]

---

[66] Eugen Weber *Apocalypses: Prophecies, Cults and Millennial Beliefs Through the Ages*, Harvard 2000.

[67] Pamela Regis *A Natural History of the Romance Novel*, Pennsylvania UP 2003.

[68] Ruth Harris *Lourdes: Body and Spirit in a Secular Age*, Allen Lane 1999.

[69] David Wengrow *The Origins of Monsters*, Princeton UP 2013 and Stephen T. Asma *On Monsters: an Unnatural History of Our Worst Fears*, Oxford UP 2010.

[70] Karen Armstrong *A Short History of Myth*, Canongate 2006, Christopher Dell *Mythology: The Complete Guide to Our Imagined Worlds*, Thames & Hudson 2012 and E.J. Michael Witzel *The Origins of the World's Mythologies*, Oxford UP 2012.

N

'NATION IS GOING TO THE DOGS' is a view favoured by opposition politicians near election time and often heeded, as a PAP. At other times it is a favourite of evangelists and those diagnosing cultural despair.

NATIVISM or 'Innatism' is used by psychologists to suggest that some ideas are pre-formed in the brain, opposing the view that it is a *Tabula Rasa* (q.v.). PAPs are not initially hard-wired in this way, but a PAP-receptive slot in the brain awaits PAPs coming from outside.

NEUROSCIENTISTS are now encouraging the idea that, with their new devices, they can explain all, and deserve bigger research grants.[71] See *fMRI*.

NEW AGE The revival in the 1970s of a life style of personal and artistic freedom, occultism and non-religious spiritualism.[72]

NOBLE SAVAGE This attractive idea, first suggested by Jean-Jacques Rousseau (1712-1778), was that remote groups existed uncorrupted by 'modern life' and lived in a natural state of health, harmony and happiness. Most claims were criticised as naïve and led to hoaxes. Margaret Mead's utopian views on Samoan life met scepticism.[73] In fiction, paradises remote from civilisation include Shangri-La.

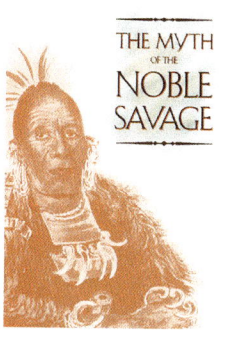

NOSTALGIA This poignant affection for the past, not always recalled accurately, is a positive emotion often triggered by key words. This includes the 'lure of the old' in the revival of older mechanical devices, artefacts and sporting equipment.

---

[71] Sally Satel and Scott O. Lilienfeld *Brainwashed: The Seductive Appeal of Mindless Neuroscience*, Basic Books 2015.

[72] James R. Lewis and J. Gordon Melton (eds) *Perspectives in the New Age* (State University of New York 1992).

[73] Ter Ellingson *The Myth of the Noble Savage*, California UP 2001.

origin story

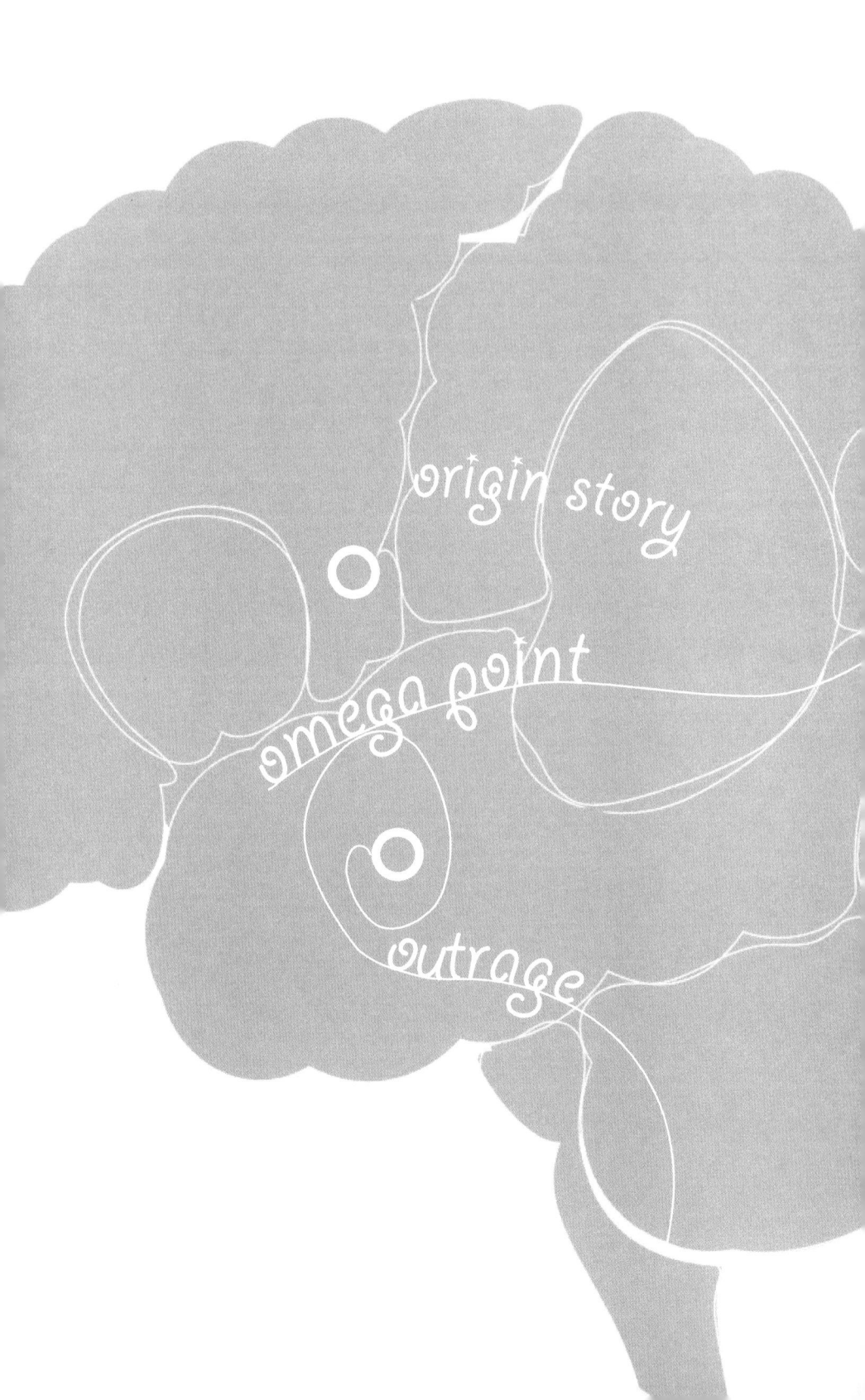

omega point

outrage

OMEGA POINT is the happy outcome for the human race predicted by the theologian Teilhard de Chardin. He suggested that man and the universe were inexorably heading to a higher final level of achievement, one close to Christ and God.

OPERATIC PAP (PLOTS) include love (often triangular), villains, betrayal, murder, cross-dressing and disguise. There are 70 operas featuring Orpheus's journey to the underworld and Faust's pact with the Devil gave 20. A related operatic PAP is that the latest production has discovered 'new meaning in the score'.

ORGAN THEFT It was widely believed in 1990s that humans were kidnapped and murdered for organ removal. Investigations instead suggested the story was an *Urban Myth* (q.v.).[74]

ORIGIN STORY, THE After any successful enterprise, it is tempting to date the inception (wrongly) back to a single moment of insight. Such attractive stories are much favoured by journalists and may be denied or only reluctantly agreed by the new hero. See also *Eureka*.

OSSIAN A highly successful Scottish literary hoax which initially fooled most of the literary world in the 1700s. The newly-discovered writer and his heroic epic poem fed the attractive view that the early Highlands of Scotland was a region of high culture. The forgery met the mood of the day elsewhere, and the many European translations were encouraged by the *Romantic Movement* (q.v.) there.[75]

OUTRAGE – a particularly unattractive, synthetic emotion favoured by journalists and politicians.

OXYGEN, see HIGH PRESSURE OXYGEN.

---

[74] Véronique Campion-Vincent *Organ Theft Legends*, Mississippi UP 2005.

[75] Thomas M. Curley *Samuel Johnson, The Ossian Fraud and the Celtic Revival*, Cambridge UP 2009.

placebo

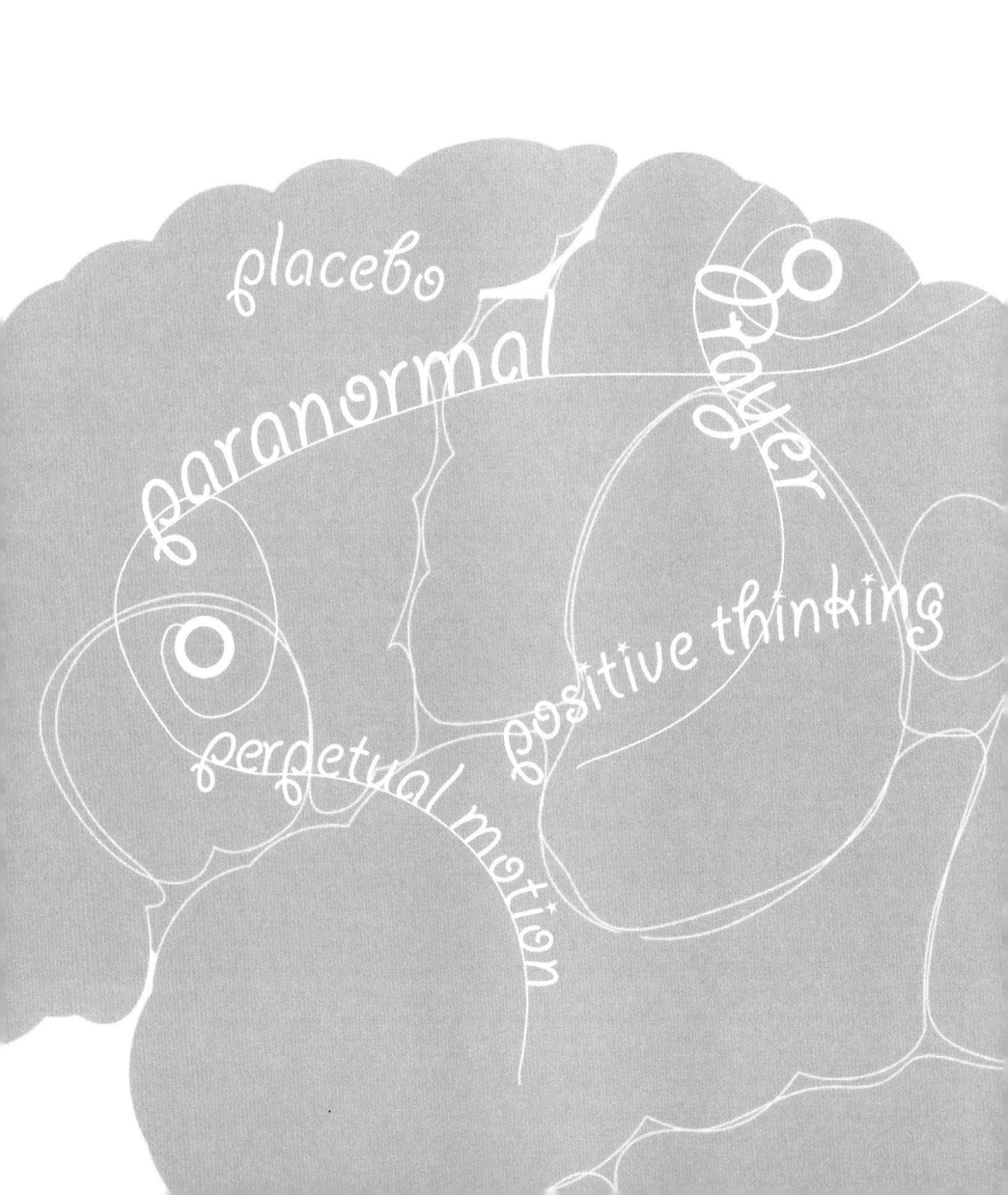

paranormal

prayer

positive thinking

perpetual motion

P

PANGLOSS, DR in Voltaire's *Candide* (1759) taught that all is for the best in this, the 'best of all possible worlds.' Panglossian optimism is a PAP favoured by some: see also *Pollyanna*.

PARADIGMS are the assumptions of the day, accepted within groups. In science, Thomas Kuhn pointed out that these are often apparently soundly-based PAPs, but are only temporary, until a 'paradigm shift' erects a new, different standpoint. See *Sheepish Tendency*.

PARADISE see *Heaven*.[76]

PARANORMAL Gallup polls show that 73% of Americans believe in at least one paranormal mechanism, a figure unchanging over many decades of polling. This is in spite of failure to detect these phenomena under controlled laboratory conditions; it has been a fruitful area for fraud. See *Telepathy*, *Clairvoyance* and *X-files*.

PARAPSYCHOLOGY (OR PSI) includes telepathy and clairvoyance.

PARTICULARLY ATTRACTIVE PLAYGROUND LORE
The Opie's classic work *The Lore and Language of Schoolchildren* (1959) showed that playtime incantations are transmitted by children to each other without coaching or adult help. The themes found and language used were unusual, yet when gathered throughout Britain, there were many similarities.

PARTICULARLY ATTRACTIVE POLITICAL slogans are chosen to resonate with the voter and hence press the right buttons. Regular choices are 'Reform' 'Openness' 'Vision' 'Hope', 'Restore Belief/Greatness' and 'Compassion'. 'Change' also has appeal and was much used by Hillary Clinton in the 2008 US primaries, then by Obama in the campaign, with David Cameron picking it up in the UK shortly after.[77]

---

[76] Allesandro Scafi *Maps of Paradise*, British Library 2013.

[77] William Safire *The New Language of Politics*, Random House 1968 and Bryan Caplan *The Myth of the Rational Voter*, Princeton UP 2008.

PARTICULARLY ATTRACTIVE PLACEBOS Inactive pills are given in 'blind' clinical trials to compare with a new active medication. The unaware patients may report that the placebos have some success. Pink placebo pills are reported to be more effective than blue ones, and fancy packaging and capsules are better than plain pills.

PENNY SHARES trading at low prices look a Particularly Attractive Punt, since moving from 5p to 7p gives a huge profit. This volatility can be exciting, also leading to huge losses, and they are usually shunned by experienced investors.

PERPETUAL MOTION The hunt is now out of favour among scientists but is not forgotten by others. Applications for such patents are still common in the US and UK. Usually these are refused, and the Patent Offices ask instead that a working model be produced.[78]

PHYSICAL EDUCATION is formal indoor sessions in a school gymnasium. In 1902 there was concern about the physique of the British nation, judged by the recruits for the Boer War. Though the explanation was the poor nutrition of the working class, physical jerks seemed an attractive alternative solution, one which was politically less sensitive.

PIRATES a favourite figure in fiction, computer games and films.[79]

PILGRIMAGE Particularly Attractive Places of Pilgrimage are less favoured in the West than before.[80] See *Lourdes*.

POLLYANNA In Eleanor Porter's 1913 novel *Pollyanna* the girl heroine highlighted the optimistic aspect of every personal situation. Psychologists identify the 'Pollyanna Principle' adopted by those who seek a positive spin, particularly on their past experience. See *Pangloss*.

PONZI SCHEMES fraudulently take investors' money and give out unusually high returns, not from investment income, but from the money arriving from new 'investors'. Of the recurring scandals, that of *Bernie Madoff's* (q.v.) $65 billion fraud is the greatest so far.[81]

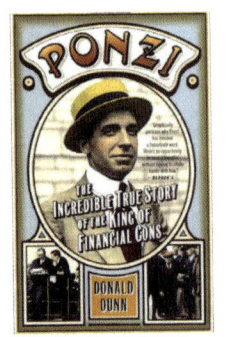

---

[78] Arthur W.J.G. Ord-Hume *Perpetual Motion: The History of an Obsession*, Adventures Unlimited Press 2015.

[79] Neil Rennie *Treasure Neverland: Real and Imaginary Pirates*, Oxford UP 2014.

[80] Robert Bartlett *Why Can the Dead Do Such Great Things? Saints and Worshippers from the Martyrs to the Reformation*, Princeton UP 2015.

[81] Tamar Frankel *The Ponzi Scheme Puzzle: A History and Analysis of Con Artists and Victims*, Oxford UP 2012.

PORN Particularly Attractive Pornography relies on short plots involving the satisfying encounters of bosses with secretaries, nurses with patients, teachers with pupils, and housewives with delivery/repair men.

POSITIVE THINKING Norman Vincent Peale (1898-1993) in his *The Power of Positive Thinking* (1952) proposed this attractive idea, alleged to lead to happiness and business success. Related to this is the current Positive Psychology movement. Claims in the *Journal of Happiness Studies* and *The Handbook of Positive Psychology* that positive thinking can improve longevity, prevent heart disease, and beat cancer have been criticised, notably by Barbara Ehrenreich.[82] See *Law of Attraction*.

POSES, ATTRACTIVE In their portraits, medical scientists were portrayed with books in the 18th century, microscopes in 19th, and in the 20th century, x-ray boxes and then computers were essential in the background.

PRAYER to a deity is used in the main religions. In illness, prayer is commonly added to medical care, offering a chance for scientific study by studying the outcome of prayer/no prayer. Those who used personal prayer usually had slightly better outcomes, but prayer by others for a patient had no effect. See Wikipedia *Studies on Intercessory Prayer*.

PRIVATE DETECTIVE an attractive literary fictional figure who, from Sherlock Holmes onwards, was a skilled investigator operating outside the national constabulary. The genre was firmly established in the 1920s by Agatha Christie, Dorothy L. Sayers and Ellery Queen and has a limited range of plots, with the culprit revealed at the last moment.[83] A niche variant is the female detective – Miss Marple and Modesty Blaise.

PROPHETS were originally those conveying messages from God(s), notably about the future.[84] Later prophets often founded their own religious cults, such as the Latter Day Saints headed by Joseph Smith from 1827. Modern-day prophets include Pat Robertson (born 1930) who from 1976 claimed to have knowledge of future events delivered to him from God. Secular prophets ('seers') have been listened to, being credited with anticipating events in their gnomic sayings. The works of the Brahan Seer in

---

[82] Barbara Ehrenreich *Smile or Die: How Positive Thinking Fooled America and the World*, Granta 2009.

[83] Julian Symons *Bloody Murder: From the Detective Story to the Crime Novel*, Grand Central Publishing 1993 and Bran Nicol *The Private Eye: Detectives in the Movies*, Reaktion 2013.

[84] Geoffrey Ashe *Encyclopedia of Prophecy*, ABC-CLIO 2001. and John F. A. Sawyer *Prophecy and the Biblical Prophets*, Oxford UP 1993.

Scotland and Nostradamus (1503-1566) in Provençal are still much admired. See *End of the World*.

PROVERBS are compact fluent statements offering wisdom derived from human events and behaviour, and these have been passed on unchanged through the centuries. Since proverbs offer rational (though sometimes contradictory) advice, they are not PAPs.

PSI see *Parapsychology*

PUBLIC RELATIONS agents seek to hit the right PAP buttons to promote their celebrity clients — lauding their nobility, charity work, survival from cancer, rehab success from drugs or alcohol problems and atonement.

PUBLISHER'S BLURB Dust jacket praise has a limited vocabulary and for non-fiction includes 'fascinating', 're-evaluation', 'newly discovered sources', 'unjustly neglected area', 'untold story', 'forgotten hero' 'myths challenged' and 'the true history'.

PYRAMID SCHEMES are a perennially attractive and unpleasant financial lure. On joining, a fee is paid to those already ahead in the scheme and if more are successfully recruited below, riches will certainly flow upwards, until the collapse. All variants are prohibited in most countries.

#	Count	
1	6	
2	36	
3	216	
4	1,296	
5	7,776	
6	46,656	
7	279,936	
8	1,679,616	
9	10,077,696	
10	60,466,176	
11	362,797,056	MORE THAN THE U.S. POPULATION
12	2,176,782,336	
13	13,060,694,016	MORE THAN THE WORLD POPULATION

Q R

QUEST a plot (or *trope* q.v.) frequently found in myths and fiction. The main character seeks a goal, which, when reached results in a lifechanging epiphany

RABBIT TO TIGER is the semi-miraculous, rapid emergence of extraordinary sporting ability. It is favoured in juvenile literature.[85]

RAGS TO RICHES a favourite trope in folk literature. The Brothers Grimm's compilation of tales popularised the well-established ancient story of Cinderella dating from the third century BC, featuring an uncaring step-mother, jealous sibs and a fairy godmother. The film 'Slumdog Millionaire' was a box office success in 2008.

RAILWAY MANIA of the mid-1840s was a *Bubble* (q.v.) following repeal of Britain's long-standing, successful, anti-speculation *Bubble Act* (1720) (q.v.). Only a 10% deposit was required on purchasing the 'Can't fail' railway stock, but by the late 1840s many shares were worthless. See *Get Rich Quick*.

RANDI, JAMES the former magician, turned to debunking paranormal claims and exposing the frauds used by mediums, spoon-benders and psychics. He is regarded as a hero by sceptical investigators.

RECOVERED/REPRESSED MEMORY Some suggest that childhood memory, particularly of unpleasant events including sexual abuse, can be forgotten, but continue to trouble the adult. 'False memories' are alleged to be implanted by probing therapists using leading questions or guided visualisation or hypnosis. This has led to 'the most acrimonious, vicious and hurtful internal debate in modern psychiatry... science, law and psychiatry have suffered.'[86]

REDEMPTION a major trope favoured by tabloid journalists and in confessional talk shows, in which past deeds are aired and forgiveness asked.

REGENCY ROMANCE fiction is based on manners and etiquette, and usually follow Jane Austen's template, including the essential happy ending.

---

[85] Tom Haliburton *Rabbit into Tiger*, Heinemann 1964.

[86] Daniel P. Brown, D. Corydon Hammond and Alan W. Scheflin *Memory, Trauma Treatment, and the Law*, Norton 1998.

REJUVENATION is the perennially attractive idea of achieving significant arrest or reversal of aging, a goal never absent, but never reached.[87]

ROMANTIC FICTION see *Mills and Boon*

ROMANTICISM was the 19th century European reaction to the rationality of the Enlightenment in the preceding century. The Romantics saw the Enlightenment as anti-religion, having shallow moral values and wrong in regarding the body as a machine. The Romantics rejected rational analysis and instead favoured emotion, feeling and *Intuition* (q.v.). See also *Brunonianism*.

RUMOURS are not PAPs or *Urban Myths* (q.v.). They spread from person to person within communities of all kinds, but when more evidence emerges, closure follows.

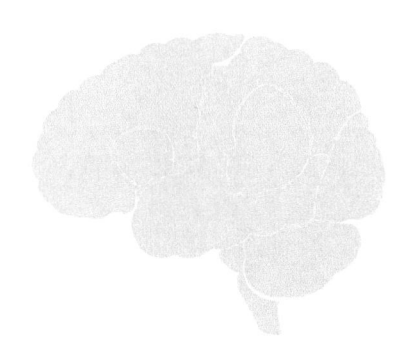

---

[87] Ted Anton *The Longevity Seekers; Science, Business and the Fountain of Youth*, Chicago UP 2013.

S

SAINTS The number of these devout holy men and women, once quite numerous on the ground, eventually peaked at about 10,000. Capable of miraculous healing when alive, they still offer posthumous intervention, and often service niche requests as a 'patron saint' dealing with specific diseases.[88]

SANTA CLAUS the saintly figure, fond of children, who in the earlier form of St Nicholas, was a gift-giver. His Christmas Eve visits with reindeer and use of chimney for entry were firmly established as a childhood PAP in the Western World in the early 1800s. The huge numbers of postal or on-line requests now made by children are dealt with sympathetically, and in the lead up to Christmas, defence agencies in North America track and announce his movements. Belief was discouraged for a while in the Soviet Union and the Eastern Block and critics of the commercialisation of Christmas point to his role; some serious-minded psychologists condemn the story as an unfortunate parental deception.[89] see *Tooth Fairy*.

SATAN see *Devil, The*

SATANIC RITUAL ABUSE was alleged to be widespread in the US in the 1980s. The 'Satanic' link was dropped first, leaving belief in widespread organised group sexual abuse, which were then not proven. Evidence often came from dubious *Recovered Memory* testimony (q.v.).[90]

SCAPEGOAT After group misfortune, it can be an attractive strategy that someone is chosen to exonerate the others. In ancient times a goat might be sacrificed for this purpose, or sent into the wilderness.[91]

SCIENTOLOGY The use of 'science' is an attractive addition to the name of any movement or belief, thus giving it authority – e.g. Christian Science.

'SCIENTISTS HAVE SHOWN ...' a standard phrase used by journalists who seldom distinguish between good and bad science. Dubious claims come from premature unpublished data, non-peer reviewed journals, and junk scientists.[92]

---

[88] Peter Brown *The Cult of the Saints*, Chicago UP 1982.
[89] Gerry Bowler *Santa Claus: A Biography*, Toronto 2007.
[90] Debbie Nathan and Michael Snedeker *Satan's Silence: Ritual Abuse and the Making of a Modern American Witch Hunt*, Basic Books 1995.
[91] Charlie Campbell *Scapegoat: A History of Blaming Other People*, Duckworth 2011.

SCOTTISH MYTHS show remarkable depth and variety. They are not restricted to folklore and legends, but extend to attractive notions on more recent matters such as the Highland clans, Scottish tartans and bagpipes.[93] See also *Loch Ness Monster*.

SECRETIVE ORGANISATIONS are vulnerable to *Conspiracy Theories* (q.v.) – e.g. that the CIA produced the HIV virus or that Britain's MI5 had a hand in Diana's death. Opinion polls show that one third of US citizens think that the federal government had a hand in 9/11.

'SEVEN BASIC PLOTS, THE' The 2004 book by Christopher Booker on story-telling concluded that there are only a limited number of fictional *Tropes* (q.v.), including The Quest, Voyage and Return, Overcoming the Monster and Rebirth. Arthur Quiller-Couch agreed that there are only seven, but other writers offer different numbers: William Foster-Harris lists only 3 plots, but Ronald Tobias gives 20 and Georges Polti identified 36.[94] See www.ipl.org

SECRET SOCIETIES exist and a particularly attractive idea is that they have an undue and menacing influence. The list includes the Freemasons, the Rosicrucians, the Bilderberg Club and Yale's student Skull and Bones society. See also *The Illuminati* and *Synarchy*.[95]

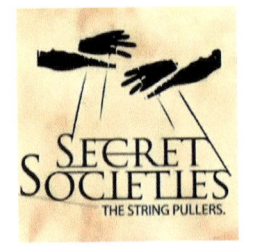

SHEEPISH TENDENCY Since most prefer to follow rather than lead, the default response is to trust and follow strong leaders in politics and business.[96] In science, most insiders find it comfortable to accept the *Paradigms* (q.v.) of the day, until these collapse. See *Confirmation Bias* and *Woozle Effect*.

SIMPSONS (THE) the longest running TV sit-com often uses and satirises PAPs – notably UFOs (q.v.), national *Stereotypes* (q.v.), *Secret Islands* (q.v.), *Conspiracy Theories* (q.v.), *Heaven and Hell* (q.v.), *Superman* (q.v.), *The Devil* (q.v.), *Santa Claus* (q.v.) and many others.

---

[92] Dan Agin *Junk Science: How Politicians, Corporations and Other Hucksters Betray Us*, Thomas Dunne 2006.

[93] Hugh Trevor-Roper *Invention of Scotland: Myth and History* Yale 2008, Alistair Campsie *The MacCrimmon Legend*, Piper's Press 1980 and Grant Jarvie *Highland Games: The Making of the Myth*, Edinburgh UP 1991.

[94] Georges Polti *The Thirty-Six Dramatic Situations* (1921).

[95] Nick Harding *Secret Societies*, Pocket Essentials 2006, Theodore Ziolkowski *Lure of the Arcane*, Hopkins 2013 and John Michael Greer *The Element Encyclopedia of Secret Societies and Hidden Histories*, Element 2006.

[96] Cass R. Sunstein *Going to Extremes: How Like Minds Unite and Divide*, OUP 2011.

SNAKE OIL originated as a sensible folk medicine treatment for skin disease, but thereafter was advocated by American itinerant healers in the early 20th century as a cure-all. The phrase is now applied to any preparation cynically marketed in spite of a known lack of effect.[97]

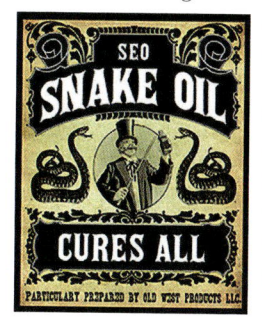

SNOW, KINDS OF
The claim that the Eskimo have a large number of words for snow, reflecting its importance in their world, was a widely believed PAP and this attractive idea underpinned much linguistic theory. When the claim was copied from book to book the count steadily increased with the re-telling. See *Woozle Effect*. But Geoffrey Pullum's polemical essay 'The Great Eskimo Vocabulary Hoax' of 1991, pointed out that the Eskimo have the usual number of words for snow and he ridiculed the scholars who had indulged in an idea too good to be false and had inflated the counts. This caused distress and amusement in academia, and the debate continues.[98]

SOAP OPERAS are successful, never-ending, television narratives based on family life and relationships in small communities. The limited *Tropes* (q.v.) include many PAPs.

'SOMETHING IN IT, PERHAPS' the sympathetic and tolerant response on hearing anecdotes about non-rational occurrences, particularly regarding clairvoyance, telepathy etc. See *Paranormal*.

SOUL, THE is believed in most religions to be the activating part of the human body which, being without substance and immortal, leaves the body after death and passes to an *Afterlife* (q.v.). Many religions believe the soul will be reunited with the body at a future resurrection of all human lives.

SOUTH SEA BUBBLE This was the most dramatic of the early financial *Bubbles* (q.v.). The South Sea Company, created in 1711, raised funds to reduce national debt, also seeking a monopoly to trade in South America, even though Spain controlled the area. Successful marketing of the stock led to speculation, with insider trading, fraud and purchases on credit, pushing the shares to ten times their value, before the collapse in 1722. *The Bubble Act* (q.v.) followed, banning 86 similar companies, and the Act was not repealed until 1825.[99] See *Extraordinary Popular Delusions*.

---

[97] Morton E. Tavel *Snake Oil is Alive and Well*, Brighton Publishing 2014.
[98] Geoffrey K. Pullum *The Great Eskimo Vocabulary Hoax*, Chicago UP 1991.
[99] Charles Mackay *Extraordinary Popular Delusions and the Madness of Crowds* London 1841.

SPINACH a particularly popular plant in popular culture, since the cartoon character Popeye the Sailor Man allegedly gained strength from the high content of iron in his favoured vegetable. Later investigation suggested that a chemist's decimal point error in 1870 was responsible for wrong iron levels.[100]

SPOON BENDING was a particularly attractive paranormal claim in the 1970s, in which cutlery was apparently deformed in plain sight by psychic power. The performance was eventually exposed by *James Randi*, the magician (q.v.), as a cynical deception, using the methods of stage magic, notably furtive action taken during brief misdirection of the watchers.[101]

STEREOTYPES are a form of PAPs, offering a simplified view of other humans beings, notably those in other nations, geographical areas or ethnic groups, or in the various professions.[102] Walter Lippmann took the term from the world of printing.

STRADIVARIUS TEST This involved six blindfolded soloists playing various violins. Three preferred the performance of a modern violin and the other three placed the Stradivarius first: the report concluded there was a 'near-canonical belief in old violins' – a PAP.[103]

SUPERHERO In fiction and comics, an ordinary youth may transform and use his added powers to release the oppressed, or even save the world from evil. It proved a successful genre from Tarzan onwards, via Superman to Spider-Man, Batman and *Wonder Woman* (q.v.).[104]

SURGEONS, EMINENT all surgeons are 'eminent' to journalists, unless when facing disciplinary proceedings.

SYNARCHY An alleged secret fascist organisation aiming to take over France prior to WW2. See *Secret Societies*.

---

[100] Glenn Cardwell (2005) 'Spinach is a good source of what? *The Skeptic* vol 25, 31-33.

[101] James Randi *The Truth About Uri Geller*, Prometheus Books 1982.

[102] Abraham Foxman *Jews and Money: The Story of a Stereotype*, Palgrave Macmillan 2010.

[103] *Proceedings of the National Academy Sciences* April 7 2014.

[104] Jill Lepore *The Secret History of Wonderwoman*, Knopf 2014.

T

TABULA RASA See *Locke, John*.

TELEPATHY is communication between human minds without any usual connection. Believed to be possible by 31% of Americans surveyed in Gallup Polls. See *Parapsychology*.

TESTOSTERONE The male sex hormone is widely and wrongly believed to be responsible for sex drive. Castration of sexual offenders is ineffective, as is TRT – Testosterone Replacement Therapy for loss of libido and the so-called male menopause. See *Rejuvenation*.

TIME TRAVEL Popularised by H.G.Wells in his *The Time Machine* (1895) it is a persistent PAP, with both forward and backward travel in time found in all the great legends. In daily life, the non-arrival of time tourists from the future has dampened such hopes.[105]

'TOO GOOD TO BE FALSE' The crucial irrational support of PAPs when first heard.[106] See particularly *Snow, Kinds of* and *Urban Myths*.

TONE (MUSCLE) is widely, but wrongly, believed to be adjustable and that it can be increased to improve physical health and athletic skills. Normal resting muscle length and contraction is not under voluntary control and cannot be changed.

TOOTH FAIRY First recorded in Norse legends from the 13th century, all cultures have rituals surrounding loss of first teeth. In the West, shed baby teeth are now placed under a pillow and, rewarded by the Tooth Fairy, payments in America now generously average $4 per tooth. All but 3% adults, looking back, when asked, cherished the childhood fantasy. See also *Santa Claus*, the other major childhood PAP.

TONSILS were formerly considered to be a design fault in the human body, and were alleged to harbour infection, and hence required removal in childhood. This PAP is now refuted and tonsils are regarded as usefully aiding the other lymphoid tissue in response to infection. See *Paradigm*.

---

[105] David Wittenberg *Time Travel*, Fordham UP 2013.

[106] J.S.Reed et al (1987) 'Too good to be false' *Sociological Inquiry* vol 57, 1-11.

TOXINS see *Detox* and *Letting the Badness Out*.

TOUCHING was the laying on of hands by the French and British Monarchs to cure disease. It was judged a particular success in the King's Evil, the tuberculous affection of the neck in children, from which spontaneous recovery was possible.[107]

TRADITION, INVENTED
The past achievements of nations or organisations, even schools, can be invented to increase status and respect. Some Scottish and Japanese national myths were invented in recent times.[108]

TROPES are the recurring literary devices and conventions that a writer can rely on to catch audience attention and raise expectations.[109] For a listing of several thousand film and literary tropes often involving PAPs, see *tvtropes.org*.

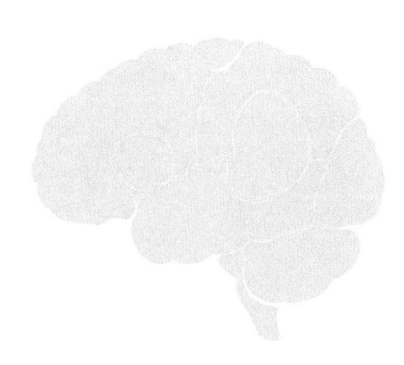

---

[107] David J. Sturdy 'The Royal Touch in England' in Heinz Duchardt et al *European Monarchy*, Stuttgart 1992.

[108] Stephen Vlastos (ed) *Mirror of Modernity: Invented Traditions of Modern Japan*, California UP 1998.

[109] John Mullan *How Novels Work*, Oxford UP 2008, Clive Bloom *Best Sellers: Popular Fiction Since 1900*, Palgrave Macmillan 2008.

U V

UFO - UNIDENTIFIED FLYING OBJECTS, a term used from 1953 by US Air Force to replace 'flying saucers', and which covered the persistent reports of mysterious objects in the sky. Explanations include visits by extraterrestrial beings, and even brief *Alien Abductions* (q.v.) into a space craft. But no physical evidence emerged nor proof of harm done. Sceptics invoke mundane explanations like weather balloons. The many negative official enquiries have encouraged *Conspiracy Theories* (q.v.) that governments are involved in a cover-up. In America, opinion polls show not only a general belief in UFOs, but also that 80% of Americans believe that their government is withholding vital information. UFOs have been a popular theme in fiction and television, and hoax claims are common.[110] See *X-files*.

UNDERDOG The unexpected success by the unfavoured in any contest, notably sport or politics, is always a PAP, and a favourite fictional *Trope* (q.v.). The 1993 film *Cool Running* featured the Winter Olympic medal-winning Jamaican bobsled team that improbably triumphed against the odds. See *David and Goliath*.

UNICORN this legendary, one-horned, exotic animal, could only be captured by a virgin, and did not exist. Huge sums were paid in early times for ground-up unicorn horn as a cure for many diseases (see *Alicorn Bubble*). Fake unicorns were exhibited in circuses, and the last expedition to find the unicorn was to Africa in the late 19th century.[111]

URBAN MYTHS/LEGENDS are new stories, too good to be false, which circulate as PAPs and gain a hold on the imagination, often with an element of humour or horror. Spread is by word of mouth among peer groups, based only on the authority of a friend of a friend, and dissemination has been broadened and accelerated by the social media, with hoaxing rife.

---

[110] Michael Shermer *Why people Believe Weird Things*, Holt 1997 and Thomas Gilovich *How We Know What Isn't So*, Free Press 1993.

[111] Chris Lavers *The Natural History of Unicorns*, Granta 2009.

New developments and analysis of such myths can be watched at the respectable, fact-checking *Snopes.com*.[112] Spreading *Memes* (q.v.) are more persistent as serious ideas of value and ephemeral *Rumours* (q.v.) quickly self-terminate. *Conspiracy Theories* (q.v.) relate to real events.

UTOPIAS Ideal communities on earth were hoped for from Plato's *Republic* and Thomas More's *Utopia* (1516) onwards.[113] Socialist thinking flirted with the idea, but without lasting involvement. Some practical success was obtained at Robert Owen's New Lanark in Scotland, but disillusionment was usual elsewhere, notably New Harmony in Indiana in the 1820s. Religious utopian communities of the early 20th century came and went, as did the hippie communes of the 1960s.

VAMPIRES John Polidori's *The Vampyre* (1819) then Bram Stoker's *Dracula* (1897) described beings who needed human blood taken from the living to survive. They remain dominant figures in horror fiction. See also *Zombies*.

VELIKOVSKY, IMMANUEL was the scientist/author of the best-selling *Worlds in Collision* (1950) which accepted the truth of Biblical events such as The Flood. He explained these past catastrophic events by the approach of planets close to the earth. He was excluded from conventional scientific circles thereafter and was seen by his supporters as a martyr.[114]

VITAMINS are essential in small quantities, and taking larger dosage seems intuitively attractive. Such treatment is controversial but has an honoured place in alternative medicine as 'orthomolecular Medicine'.

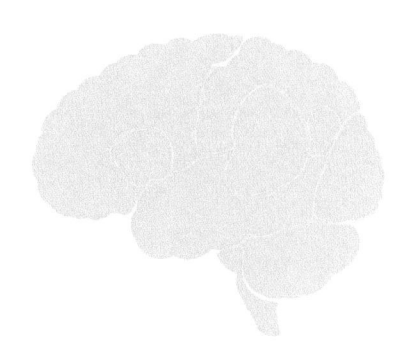

---

[112] Philip Ward *A Dictionary of Common Fallacies*, Oleander Press 1978 and Jan Harold Brunvand *Too Good to be True: The Colossal Book of Urban Legends*, Norton 1999.

[113] R.C.S.Trahair *Utopias and Utopians: An Historical Dictionary*, Greenwood 1999.

[114] Michael D. Gordin *The Pseudoscience Wars: Immanuel Velikovsky and the Birth of the Modern Fringe*, Chicago UP 2012.

WATER There is a profound, ancient belief in the healing powers and beneficence of water. Holy waters from springs and rivers could heal and baptismal water could bless. As the belief in magical healing declined the value of springs with water containing chemicals followed and when these spas fell out of favour, the pure water at the hydropathics was applied outside or inside.

WESTERN, THE This film genre was the dominant Hollywood theme of the 1950s. Set in the lawless 'Wild' American Old West 1850-1900, stock characters were cowboys, Indians, outlaws and hardpressed, ineffective sheriffs who all saw action in decayed townships with a saloon and jail house. The wandering hero arrives and single-handedly uses his wits to right wrongs and rescue ladies in distress, with good triumphing over evil in the end, which usually features a gunfight.[115] See *Arthurian Legend* and *Underdog*.

'WE WERE ROBBED' is an attractive and reassuring verdict on a team's sporting loss, explaining that unfair circumstances decided the outcome.

WHIG INTERPRETATION OF HISTORY was identified in Herbert Butterfield's 1931 book of that name which criticised some historians' attractive view that the human world is on an steady path of progress towards enlightenment. This stance meant ignoring periods of adversity and hesitation, particularly in politics and science, to create instead a comforting narrative of onwards and ever-upwards progress.

WITCHES Their existence was widely supported in the Western thought until the 1700s, and witchcraft is still a lively concept in developing cultures.[116] Gallup Polls show that 21% of Americans still believe in witches.

WITCH HUNT Modified forms of the earlier witch hunts regularly appear in which there is short-term irrational persecution of the innocent.[117] See *Satanic Ritual Abuse*.

---

[115] David Hamilton Murdoch *The American West: The Invention of a Myth*, Nevada UP 2001.

[116] Marion Gibson *Witchcraft and Society in England and America, 1550-1750*, Cornell UP 2003.

[117] Robert Rapley *Witch Hunts: from Salem to Guantanamo Bay*, McGll UP 2007 and John Demos *The Enemy Within: 2,000 Years of Witch-Hunting in the Western World*, Viking 2008.

WIZARD The stock character who regularly helps sell popular fiction books.[118]

WOMENS' FASHION is regularly seen as a threat to health – tight corsets (damages kidneys), high heels (cause Morton's neuromas in the foot), winkle-picker shoes (give ingrowing toenails). These easy allegations are not evidence-based.

WONDER WOMAN is the nubile female in American comics and films. She uses superhuman powers, plus the Lasso of Truth, to fight many enemies and bring in a Better Society, including gender equality. See *Superhero*.

WOOZLE EFFECT is a term introduced by William Bevan, in which an unreliable written claim is then quoted by subsequent writers, and, often simplified and made more vivid, it thus becomes established as fact. These, also called 'factoids', are often PAPs. The Woozle was hunted by Winnie-the-Pooh and his friends, who set off in the snow, but turning in a circle, mistakenly followed their own footsteps.[119] This Effect is the scholarly version of the *Urban Myth* (q.v.).

WRESTLING (PROFESSIONAL) This older competitive sport morphed into entertainment with stage-managed pantomimes instead, displaying suffering, near defeat, but final victory and justice. The many subplots include cheating, the rescue of downed comrades by colleagues, dramatic entries and use of the ropes, with the high profile role of the (sometimes crooked) referees. The audiences suspend disbelief to enjoy a vivid choreographed world of Goodies and Baddies, as in a morality play.[120]

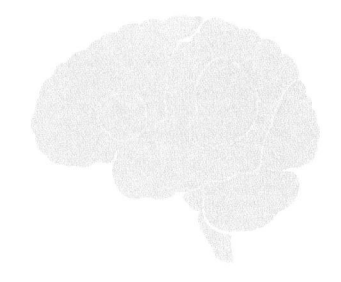

---

[118] John Matthews *Wizards: The Quest for the Wizard from Merlin to Harry Potter*, Barrons 2003.
[119] William Bevan *Modern Psychologists: Scientific Woozle Hunters?* Munksgaard 1953.
[120] Sharon Mazer *Professional Wrestling: Sport and Spectacle*, Mississippi UP 1998.

X Y Z

X-FILES This American television series, the longest-running science fiction series, featured many PAPs, notably UFOs (q.v.), *Urban Myths* (q.v.), *Secret Societies* (q.v.) and the *Paranormal* (q.v.). The main characters were involved in a serious dialogue combining belief and scepticism.[121]

ZEITGEIST the mood and assumptions of the times, particularly in intellectual life, politics, industry and the arts. In retrospect it always incorporated many PAPs of the day.

ZOMBIES are the reanimated dead, which feature in horror films and fiction. George Romero's 1968 film re-established interest in the zombie, as representing cultural decline.[122] See also *Vampire*.

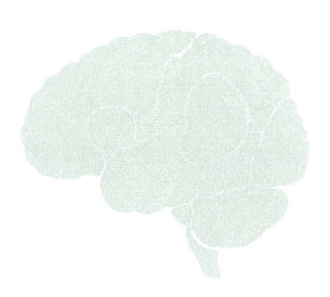

---

[121] Dean A. Kowalski *The Philosophy of the X-files*, Kentucky UP 2007.

[122] Roger Luckhurst *Zombies: A Cultural History* Reaktion, London 2015.

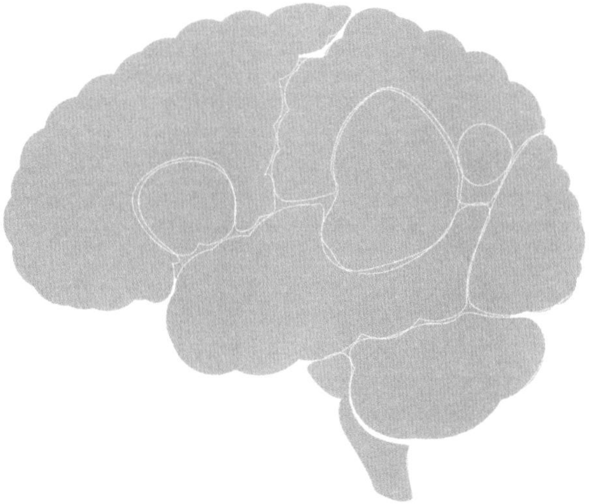

Made in the USA
Charleston, SC
17 April 2016